New Perspectives on Transformative Leadership in Education

By

Shashikant Nishant Sharma

Research Head, Track2Training, New Delhi, India

&

Moses Adeleke Adeoye

Al-Hikmah University Ilorin, Nigeria

Published by

Edupedia Publications Pvt Ltd, New Delhi

www.edupub.org

ISBN: **978-93-92585-26-5**

DOI: **https://doi.org/ 10.5281/zenodo.10970922**

Edition: **First**

Imprint: **EduPub**

Year: **2024**

Publisher: **Edupedia Publications Pvt Ltd**, New Delhi

Table of Contents

Preface of the Book

In the ever-evolving landscape of education, leadership plays a pivotal role in shaping the experiences and outcomes of learners, educators, and communities. The need for transformative leadership in education has never been more pressing as we stand at the threshold of a new era, marked by rapid technological advancements, societal changes, and global interconnectedness.

This book, "New Perspectives on Transformative Leadership in Education," emerges as a response to the complex challenges and opportunities facing educational leaders today. Drawing upon the collective wisdom and expertise of scholars, practitioners, and thought leaders in the field, this volume offers fresh insights, innovative approaches, and practical strategies to inspire and empower educational leaders in their quest for positive change.

Through diverse perspectives, ranging from theoretical frameworks to real-world case studies, this book explores the multifaceted nature of transformative leadership and its impact on educational institutions, systems, and cultures. From fostering inclusive environments to harnessing the potential of technology, from promoting equity and social justice to nurturing collaborative partnerships, the chapters within this book delve into the key dimensions of transformative leadership and its implications for creating meaningful and sustainable change in education.

Each chapter in this volume is a testament to the dedication and passion of educators and leaders who are committed to reimagining the possibilities of education and unlocking the full potential of every learner. By challenging conventional wisdom, embracing innovation, and fostering a culture of continuous learning and improvement, transformative leaders have the power to ignite positive transformations that resonate far beyond the confines of the classroom.

As editors, we are deeply grateful to all the contributors who have generously shared their insights and experiences, enriching this volume with diverse perspectives and valuable insights. We hope this book will serve as a catalyst for dialogue, reflection, and action, inspiring educational leaders to embark on their own transformative journeys and create a brighter future for learners around the globe.

May this book serve as a beacon of inspiration and guidance for all those who strive to lead with vision, courage, and compassion in the pursuit of excellence and equity in education.

Chapter 1: Introduction

Transformative leadership is a style of leadership that focuses on creating significant change or transformation within an organization or community (Mitra & Sinha, 2023). It goes beyond traditional forms of leadership that primarily aim to maintain the status quo or make incremental improvements. Instead, transformative leaders inspire and empower others to envision and achieve ambitious goals, often by challenging existing norms, fostering innovation, and promoting personal growth and development.

Here are some key characteristics and principles of transformative leadership:

Visionary Thinking: Transformative leaders have a clear and compelling vision for the future of their organization or community. They communicate this vision in a way that inspires and motivates others to join them in pursuing it.

Inspiration and Empowerment: These leaders empower their followers by instilling confidence, trust, and autonomy. They encourage others to think critically, take initiative, and contribute their unique talents and perspectives to achieve common goals.

Intellectual Stimulation: Transformative leaders stimulate creativity and innovation by challenging assumptions, encouraging intellectual curiosity, and promoting a culture of continuous learning and improvement.

Ethical and Moral Leadership: They adhere to high ethical standards and act with integrity, fairness, and transparency. They prioritize the well-being and interests of their followers and the broader community over personal gain.

Emotional Intelligence: Transformative leaders possess strong emotional intelligence, enabling them to empathize with others, build meaningful relationships, and effectively manage conflicts and challenges.

Risk-taking and Resilience: They are willing to take calculated risks and embrace uncertainty in pursuit of their vision. They demonstrate resilience in the face of setbacks and failures, using them as opportunities for learning and growth.

Collaboration and Inclusivity: Transformative leaders foster a collaborative and inclusive environment where diverse perspectives are valued and leveraged to drive innovation and problem-solving.

Continuous Learning and Adaptation: They are lifelong learners who continuously seek new knowledge and insights to adapt to changing circumstances and emerging challenges.

Transformational Impact: Ultimately, transformative leaders bring about positive and sustainable change that transcends the organization or community, leaving a lasting legacy of growth, empowerment, and social impact.

Transformative leadership can be applied in various contexts, including business, politics, education, and community development, where the need for profound change and innovation is paramount. In the educational landscape, transformative leadership plays a crucial role in driving positive change and innovation, both at the institutional level and in the broader educational community. Here are some key reasons why transformative leadership is significant in education:

Visionary Leadership: Transformative leaders in education articulate a compelling vision for the future of their institutions, focusing on improving student outcomes, fostering a culture of academic excellence, and addressing the evolving needs of learners in the 21st century.

Promotion of Equity and Inclusion: Transformative leaders prioritize equity and inclusion, advocating for equal access to quality education for all students, regardless of their background, socio-economic status, or abilities. They work to dismantle barriers to learning and create inclusive learning environments where every student feels valued and supported.

Innovation and Creativity: Transformative leaders encourage innovation and creativity in teaching and learning, leveraging technology, interdisciplinary approaches, and experiential learning opportunities to engage students and enhance their educational experiences. They promote a culture of experimentation and risk-taking among educators, encouraging them to explore new teaching methods and strategies (Bhatia et al., 2015).

Professional Development and Growth: Transformative leaders invest in the professional development and growth of educators, providing opportunities for ongoing learning, collaboration, and mentorship. They empower teachers to take ownership of their professional practice, supporting them in acquiring new skills, refining their teaching techniques, and staying abreast of emerging trends and research in education (Dowling, 2016).

Community Engagement and Partnerships: Transformative leaders recognize the importance of community engagement and partnerships in enriching the educational experience and expanding opportunities for students. They collaborate with parents, community organizations, businesses, and other stakeholders to create meaningful learning experiences both inside and outside the classroom.

Data-Informed Decision Making: Transformative leaders use data to inform their decision-making processes, leveraging assessment data, student performance metrics, and other quantitative and qualitative indicators to identify areas for improvement, monitor progress, and make informed policy and resource allocation decisions. Transformative leaders cultivate leadership capacity at all levels of the educational system, empowering teachers, administrators, and other stakeholders to become change agents and leaders in their own right. They foster a culture of distributed leadership, where decision-making authority and responsibility are shared among various stakeholders, promoting collective ownership and accountability for achieving organizational goals.

Adaptation to Changing Demands: Transformative leaders are adaptable and responsive to changing educational demands and external pressures, whether they be technological advancements, shifts in student demographics, or evolving policy landscapes. They anticipate future challenges and opportunities, proactively seeking innovative solutions to address them and position their institutions for success in a rapidly changing world (Asurakkody & Kim, 2020). In summary, transformative leadership in education is significant because it fosters visionary leadership, promotes equity and inclusion, encourages innovation and creativity, supports professional development and growth, facilitates community engagement and partnerships, informs data-driven decision making, cultivates leadership capacity, and enables adaptation to changing demands. By embodying these principles, transformative leaders contribute to the creation of thriving learning communities where all students have the opportunity to reach their full potential.

Chapter 2: Historical Evolution of Educational Leadership

The evolution of educational leadership can be understood through several historical phases, each influenced by societal, cultural, and educational trends. While the specifics may vary across regions and time periods, the following overview provides a general outline of the historical evolution of educational leadership:

Ancient Civilizations (Pre-500 BCE):

Leadership in education was often associated with religious or political authority. In ancient civilizations such as Mesopotamia, Egypt, Greece, and China, educational leadership was primarily the domain of priests, scribes, or elite scholars who were responsible for transmitting knowledge and cultural values to future generations (McIntosh, 2008).

During the ancient civilizations preceding 500 BCE, educational leadership was deeply intertwined with religious and political authority structures. In Mesopotamia, the cradle of civilization, educational institutions such as temples and palaces served as centers of learning, where priests and scribes held significant influence as educational leaders. These religious figures were not only responsible for administering spiritual rites but also for imparting knowledge of mathematics, astronomy, literature, and law to the next generation.

Similarly, in ancient Egypt, educational leadership was closely tied to the divine order, with the pharaohs and priestly caste playing pivotal roles in overseeing educational institutions such as the scribal schools. Scribes, who were educated in specialized schools, held esteemed positions in society and were entrusted with recording historical events, maintaining administrative records, and transmitting cultural knowledge through writing (Dehalwar & Sharma, 2023).

In ancient Greece, educational leadership took on a more philosophical and humanistic dimension, particularly during the Classical period. Influential figures such as Plato, Aristotle, and Socrates were not only revered as scholars but also as mentors and guides to aspiring intellectuals. Philosophical schools, such as Plato's Academy and Aristotle's Lyceum, served as centers of intellectual inquiry and moral education, where students engaged in dialectical discussions, contemplation of ethical principles, and the pursuit of truth and wisdom.

In China, educational leadership was deeply rooted in Confucian philosophy, which emphasized the importance of education in cultivating moral character, social harmony, and filial piety. Confucian scholars, known as literati, played key roles as educators and mentors, guiding students in the study of classical texts, ethical principles, and proper conduct. Educational institutions such as the Imperial Academy (Taixue) served as training grounds for aspiring bureaucrats, who were expected to uphold Confucian values and serve the state with integrity and wisdom (Hansen et al., 2022).

Across these ancient civilizations, educational leadership was characterized by a reverence for tradition, a focus on moral and intellectual development, and a close association with religious or political authority. Educational leaders, whether priests, scribes, philosophers, or scholars, were entrusted with the sacred task of transmitting knowledge, preserving cultural heritage, and shaping the minds and values of future generations. Their influence extended far beyond the classroom, shaping the fabric of society and the course of history for centuries to come.

Classical Period (500 BCE - 500 CE):

With the emergence of philosophical schools in ancient Greece, such as those founded by Plato and Aristotle, educational leadership began to emphasize the cultivation of moral character, critical thinking, and civic virtue. Philosophers and scholars played key roles as educational leaders, guiding students in the pursuit of intellectual and ethical development.

During the Classical Period, spanning from 500 BCE to 500 CE, educational leadership underwent significant transformations, particularly in ancient Greece, where the emergence of philosophical schools revolutionized educational practices and ideals.

In ancient Greece, the city-states were vibrant centers of intellectual and cultural exchange, fostering the development of philosophical thought and educational innovation. Prominent philosophers such as Plato and Aristotle founded influential schools of philosophy, such as the Academy and the Lyceum, which served as hubs for intellectual inquiry and moral education.

Under the guidance of these philosophical leaders, educational institutions shifted their focus from rote memorization and practical skills to the cultivation of moral character, critical thinking, and civic virtue. Philosophers emphasized the importance of questioning assumptions, engaging in dialectical dialogue, and seeking knowledge for its own sake, rather than for utilitarian purposes.

Educational leadership during this period was characterized by a deep commitment to the holistic development of the individual, encompassing both intellectual and moral dimensions. Philosophers served as mentors and guides, inspiring students to explore the fundamental questions of existence, the nature of reality, and the meaning of life (Aagaard & Earnest, 2021).

In addition to philosophical schools, the gymnasiums and academies of ancient Greece provided physical and intellectual training for young men, preparing them for active participation in civic life. Educational leaders, including gymnasiarchs and rhetoricians, oversaw the curriculum and pedagogical practices, promoting physical fitness, rhetorical skills, and ethical conduct among students.

The influence of Greek educational ideals spread throughout the Mediterranean world, influencing educational practices in neighboring regions such as Rome and Egypt. Following the conquests of Alexander the Great, the Hellenistic period saw the spread of Greek language, culture, and educational philosophy across vast territories, further shaping the intellectual landscape of the ancient world (Arkin et al., 2019).

Overall, the Classical Period marked a turning point in the history of educational leadership, as philosophical schools emerged as centers of intellectual and moral education, challenging traditional notions of knowledge and authority. Philosophers and scholars played pivotal roles as educational leaders, guiding students in the pursuit of truth, wisdom, and virtue, and laying the foundation for the development of Western educational traditions.

Medieval and Renaissance Eras (500 - 1500 CE):

During the Middle Ages, educational leadership was closely tied to religious institutions, particularly in Europe, where monastic and cathedral schools were established to educate clergy and nobility. With the Renaissance, there was a revival of interest in classical learning and humanistic education, led by scholars such as Erasmus and the rise of universities as centers of intellectual inquiry.

During the Medieval and Renaissance Eras (500 - 1500 CE), educational leadership underwent significant transformations, closely intertwined with the socio-political and cultural developments of the time.

In the Middle Ages, educational leadership was predominantly shaped by the influence of religious institutions, particularly within Europe. Monastic and cathedral schools emerged as vital centers of learning, primarily tasked with educating the clergy and nobility. These institutions played a pivotal role in preserving knowledge, with a curriculum heavily focused on theology, philosophy, and Latin. Educational leadership within these settings was often carried out by clergy members, who not only imparted knowledge but also wielded considerable authority within their communities. However, the Renaissance period brought about a profound shift in educational leadership and philosophy. This era witnessed a revival of interest in classical learning, sparked by the rediscovery of ancient texts and manuscripts. Humanistic education emerged as a prominent movement, emphasizing the study of literature, history, and the arts, in addition to traditional theological subjects. Scholars such as Erasmus championed this humanistic approach, advocating for a more well-rounded and practical education (Knudsen, 2016).

The rise of universities as centers of intellectual inquiry further propelled educational leadership into new realms. Universities, such as those in Bologna, Paris, and Oxford, became hubs of learning, attracting students and scholars from across Europe. These institutions fostered academic freedom and encouraged critical thinking, laying the groundwork for the development of modern academia. Educational leadership during the Renaissance was characterized by the patronage of rulers, aristocrats, and wealthy merchants who supported the arts and sciences. These patrons played a crucial role in funding educational institutions and sponsoring scholars, fostering an environment conducive to intellectual exploration and innovation. Overall, the Medieval and Renaissance Eras witnessed a dynamic evolution in educational leadership, from the dominance of religious institutions to the emergence of humanistic ideals and the establishment of universities as bastions of knowledge and inquiry. This period laid the foundation for modern educational practices and institutions, shaping the course of intellectual history for centuries to come.

Enlightenment and Industrial Revolution (17th - 19th centuries):

The Enlightenment period saw the emergence of secular educational institutions and the spread of literacy and scientific knowledge. Educational leadership increasingly focused on rationality, empiricism, and the cultivation of critical thinking skills. With the Industrial Revolution, the expansion of formal schooling and the rise of mass education systems led to the professionalization of educational leadership roles, including school principals and superintendents.

During the Enlightenment period (17th - 19th centuries), significant shifts in educational leadership occurred, driven by the era's intellectual movements and socio-economic changes. This period marked a departure from the dominance of religious institutions in education towards secular institutions, fostering the spread of literacy, scientific knowledge, and the principles of rationality and empiricism.

A growing emphasis on the cultivation of critical thinking skills and the dissemination of knowledge beyond the confines of religious doctrine characterized educational leadership during the Enlightenment. Secular educational institutions, such as public schools and academies, began to emerge, providing education to a wider segment of society. These institutions focused on subjects such as mathematics, natural sciences, literature, and philosophy, aiming to equip students with the tools for independent inquiry and intellectual exploration (Clarke & Harvey, 1991).

Enlightenment thinkers, such as Voltaire, Rousseau, and John Locke, advocated for educational reforms that emphasized reason, tolerance, and the importance of individual freedom. Their ideas influenced educational leadership practices, leading to the development of curricula that promoted intellectual curiosity and the development of moral character.

The Industrial Revolution further reshaped educational leadership by necessitating the expansion of formal schooling to meet the demands of an increasingly industrialized society. With the rise of factories and urbanization, there was a growing need for a literate and skilled workforce. Mass education systems were established to provide basic education to the general populace, leading to the proliferation of elementary schools and the standardization of curricula (Hartati & Muktar, 2019).

The professionalization of educational leadership roles also occurred during this period, with the emergence of school principals, superintendents, and educational administrators. These leaders were tasked with managing the increasingly complex education systems, overseeing curriculum development, teacher training, and school operations. The establishment of educational standards and regulations became essential as education became more institutionalized and centralized (Burns et al., 2019).

Overall, the Enlightenment and Industrial Revolution period witnessed a transformation in educational leadership, marked by the rise of secular educational institutions, the spread of literacy and scientific knowledge, and the professionalization of educational roles. These developments laid the groundwork for modern educational systems and the continued evolution of educational leadership practices.

Progressive Era (late 19th - early 20th centuries):

The Progressive movement in education, led by figures such as John Dewey, emphasized experiential learning, child-centered pedagogy, and social reform. Educational leaders sought to create more democratic and inclusive schools that met the diverse needs of students and promoted active engagement in learning.

During the Progressive Era, spanning the late 19th to the early 20th centuries, profound changes swept through educational leadership, driven by a desire for reform, social justice, and innovation in schooling. At the forefront of this movement stood influential figures like John Dewey, whose ideas reshaped educational philosophy and practice.

A shift towards experiential learning and child-centered pedagogy characterized the Progressive movement in education. Progressive educators believed that learning should be meaningful, relevant, and rooted in the experiences of students. John Dewey, often regarded as the father of progressive education, advocated for hands-on learning experiences that encouraged critical thinking, problem-solving, and collaboration. Dewey's philosophy emphasized the integration of subjects, project-based learning, and the importance of connecting classroom learning to real-world contexts (Stone et al., 2018).

Educational leaders during the Progressive Era sought to create more democratic and inclusive schools that recognized the diverse needs and backgrounds of students. They promoted active engagement in learning, viewing education as a means of empowering individuals and fostering social change. Progressive educators emphasized the importance of social justice, equity, and the promotion of democratic values within educational institutions (Ali et al., 2021).

As part of their efforts to reform education, Progressive leaders advocated for changes in curriculum, assessment, and school organization. They introduced innovative teaching methods, such as group work, cooperative learning, and experiential activities, to create dynamic and interactive learning environments. Curriculum reforms aimed to make learning more relevant and connected to students' lives, while assessment practices shifted towards assessing students' understanding and abilities rather than rote memorization.

The Progressive Era also saw the emergence of new educational initiatives, such as the establishment of kindergarten programs, vocational schools, and community-based education projects. Educational leaders worked to expand access to schooling and improve the quality of education for all students, regardless of their socio-economic background or abilities.

Overall, the Progressive Era represented a period of significant transformation in educational leadership, characterized by a commitment to experiential learning, social reform, and the promotion of democratic ideals. The ideas and practices introduced during this period continue to influence educational philosophy and practice to this day, shaping the way we think about teaching, learning, and leadership in education.

Post-World War II Era (mid-20th century):

The post-World War II period saw the expansion of educational access and the rise of educational psychology and organizational theory. Educational leadership increasingly drew on insights from psychology, sociology, and management theory to inform practices such as instructional leadership, curriculum development, and school management.

The post-World War II era, spanning the mid-20th century, brought about significant changes in educational leadership, driven by the imperatives of rebuilding societies and advancing education as a tool for social and economic progress. This period witnessed a rapid expansion of educational access and the emergence of new theories and practices that reshaped educational leadership.

One of the defining features of this era was the widespread expansion of educational access at all levels. Governments around the world recognized the importance of education in rebuilding post-war societies and fostering economic development. As a result, there was a concerted effort to increase enrollment rates, build new schools, and improve infrastructure. Educational leadership played a crucial role in coordinating these efforts, overseeing the expansion of educational systems and ensuring equitable access to schooling for all segments of society (James & Salahou, 2021).

Another significant development during this period was the rise of educational psychology and organizational theory as influential fields in educational leadership. Drawing on insights from psychology, sociology, and management theory, educational leaders began to adopt more scientific and evidence-based approaches to educational practice. Educational psychology provided valuable insights into how students learn and develop, informing teaching methods, curriculum design, and assessment practices. Organizational theory, meanwhile, offered frameworks for understanding the complex dynamics of educational institutions and improving school management and leadership.

During the post-World War II era, educational leadership increasingly focused on concepts such as instructional leadership, curriculum development, and school improvement. Educational leaders were expected to manage administrative tasks and provide instructional guidance and support to teachers, fostering a culture of continuous improvement and innovation in teaching and learning. Curriculum development became a key area of focus, with educational leaders working to design curriculum responsive to students' needs and reflective of societal values and goals (Aagaard et al., 2018).

The post-World War II era also witnessed the professionalization of educational leadership roles, with the establishment of formal training programs and credentialing requirements for school administrators. Educational leaders were expected to possess a blend of academic knowledge, practical skills, and leadership abilities, enabling them to effectively navigate the complexities of educational systems and drive positive change within schools and communities. Overall, the post-World War II era was a period of significant growth and evolution in educational leadership, marked by the expansion of educational access, the emergence of new theories and practices, and the professionalization of leadership roles. The insights and innovations that emerged during this period continue to shape educational leadership practices and policies today, as educators strive to meet the ever-changing needs of students and society.

Civil Rights Movement and Accountability Era (mid-20th century to present):

The Civil Rights Movement and subsequent social justice movements brought attention to issues of equity, diversity, and inclusion in education. Educational leadership became more focused on promoting social justice, addressing disparities in educational outcomes, and ensuring access to quality education for all students. The accountability era, marked by increased standardized testing and accountability measures, led to greater emphasis on data-driven decision making and school improvement efforts (Bonomi, 2019).

The Civil Rights Movement, which gained momentum in the mid-20th century and subsequent social justice movements, profoundly influenced educational leadership by bringing issues of equity, diversity, and inclusion to the forefront of educational discourse. Educational leaders increasingly became champions for social justice, striving to address disparities in educational outcomes and ensure equitable access to quality education for all students.

During this era, educational leadership underwent a transformational shift towards promoting equity and inclusivity in schools. Leaders recognized the importance of acknowledging and addressing systemic inequalities that marginalized certain groups of students, particularly those from minority backgrounds. They advocated for policies and practices aimed at dismantling discriminatory barriers to education and creating more inclusive learning environments.

Educational leaders played crucial roles in implementing desegregation efforts, ensuring that schools became more diverse and equitable spaces for all students. They worked to eliminate discriminatory practices such as segregation, unequal funding, and tracking, and promoted policies that fostered diversity, multiculturalism, and inclusivity (Allen, 2019).

Furthermore, the accountability era, which emerged alongside the Civil Rights Movement, introduced new challenges and priorities for educational leadership. Increased standardized testing and accountability measures placed greater emphasis on data-driven decision-making and school improvement efforts. Educational leaders were tasked with analyzing student performance data, identifying areas for improvement, and implementing evidence-based strategies to enhance teaching and learning outcomes. During the accountability era, educational leadership also focused on fostering a culture of continuous improvement and accountability within schools. Leaders implemented systems for monitoring and evaluating teacher effectiveness, curriculum alignment, and overall school performance to ensure that all students received a high-quality education. In summary, the Civil Rights Movement and the accountability era have significantly shaped educational leadership by placing a greater emphasis on equity, diversity, and accountability. Educational leaders have played instrumental roles in advancing social justice initiatives, promoting inclusive educational practices, and ensuring that all students have access to the resources and opportunities needed to succeed.

Globalization and Technological Advancements (late 20th century to present):

The globalization of education and rapid advancements in technology have transformed the landscape of educational leadership. Leaders are increasingly called upon to navigate complex challenges such as globalization, digitalization, and demographic shifts, while promoting innovation, collaboration, and lifelong learning in educational settings.

In the late 20th century and continuing into the present, globalization and technological advancements have profoundly influenced educational leadership, reshaping the way leaders approach their roles and responsibilities. The interconnectedness brought about by globalization, coupled with rapid advancements in technology, has transformed the landscape of education, presenting both opportunities and challenges for educational leaders. Globalization has expanded the reach of education, allowing for greater collaboration and exchange of ideas across borders. Educational leaders are now tasked with navigating the complexities of a globalized world, fostering cultural understanding, and preparing students to thrive in diverse and interconnected societies. They must promote global citizenship, intercultural competence, and an appreciation for diverse perspectives within educational settings.

Technological advancements have revolutionized teaching and learning, providing new tools and platforms for educational leaders to enhance instruction, communication, and collaboration. Educational leaders are increasingly leveraging technology to personalize learning experiences, engage students, and expand access to education through online and distance learning initiatives. They must stay abreast of emerging technologies and trends, ensuring that schools are equipped to adapt to the digital age and harness the potential of technology to improve educational outcomes (Brown, 2013). Moreover, globalization and technological advancements have led to demographic shifts and changing student populations, presenting unique challenges for educational leaders. Leaders must address issues of equity, diversity, and inclusion, ensuring that educational opportunities are accessible to all students, regardless of their backgrounds or circumstances. They must promote inclusive practices, create culturally responsive learning environments, and support marginalized groups to thrive academically and socially (Brahma, 2019).

Educational leaders are also called upon to foster innovation and creativity in education, encouraging experimentation, risk-taking, and entrepreneurial thinking. They must cultivate a culture of innovation within schools, empowering teachers and students to explore new ideas, solve complex problems, and adapt to a rapidly changing world. Educational leaders play a critical role in leading change, facilitating collaboration, and driving continuous improvement in educational practices and policies.

In summary, globalization and technological advancements have redefined the role of educational leadership, requiring leaders to navigate the complexities of a globalized, digital world while promoting innovation, collaboration, and inclusivity in educational settings. Leaders must embrace change, adapt to new challenges, and harness the transformative power of education to prepare students for success in the 21st century.

Throughout its history, educational leadership has evolved in response to changing societal needs and educational paradigms, reflecting broader shifts in philosophy, politics, and culture. Today, educational leaders are tasked with addressing complex challenges and opportunities in a rapidly changing world, while upholding the values of equity, inclusion, and excellence in education.

Traditional Leadership Models

Traditional leadership models encompass a range of approaches to leadership that have been historically prevalent in various contexts. These models often emphasize hierarchical structures, clear lines of authority, and top-down decision-making. While they may vary in their specific characteristics and applications, traditional leadership models generally prioritize stability, order, and efficiency within organizations. Some of the most prominent traditional leadership models include:

Autocratic Leadership: In this model, the leader holds all the decision-making power and authority, with little input from subordinates. Decisions are made unilaterally, and directives are communicated downward. Autocratic leaders often rely on their own judgment and expertise to guide the organization, and they may enforce strict control over their followers (Aarons et al., 2016).

Transactional Leadership: Transactional leaders focus on establishing clear expectations and providing rewards or punishments based on performance. This model relies on the exchange of rewards, such as salary increases or promotions, for meeting predetermined goals and objectives.

Transactional leaders monitor performance closely and intervene when necessary to ensure compliance with established standards.

Bureaucratic Leadership: Bureaucratic leadership is characterized by adherence to formal rules, procedures, and regulations. Leaders in bureaucratic organizations rely on standardized processes and hierarchical structures to maintain order and control. Decision-making authority is typically centralized, and individuals are assigned specific roles and responsibilities based on their position within the hierarchy.

Charismatic Leadership: Charismatic leaders inspire and motivate followers through their personal charisma, vision, and persuasive communication skills. They often possess a strong presence and are able to rally others around a shared vision or mission. Charismatic leaders may rely on their charisma and charm to influence others, rather than formal authority or rules.

Authoritarian Leadership: Authoritarian leaders exercise strict control over their followers and demand unquestioning obedience. They may use fear, intimidation, or coercion to maintain power and authority. Authoritarian leaders make decisions independently and expect compliance from their subordinates without question (Lu et al., 2019).

These traditional leadership models have been widely studied and practiced in various organizational settings, although they are increasingly being challenged and supplemented by more contemporary approaches to leadership, such as transformational leadership, servant leadership, and adaptive leadership. While traditional leadership models may offer stability and predictability in certain contexts, they can also be rigid and inflexible, limiting innovation and adaptability in rapidly changing environments. As organizations evolve and face new challenges, leaders must be open to exploring alternative models and approaches to effectively meet the needs of their followers and achieve organizational goals.

Shifts and Trends in Educational Leadership

Shifts and trends in educational leadership reflect the evolving needs, challenges, and opportunities within the field of education. These shifts are influenced by various factors, including changes in technology, demographics, social and economic conditions, as well as advancements in educational research and theory. Some of the key shifts and trends in educational leadership include:

Emphasis on Equity and Inclusion: There is a growing recognition of the importance of equity, diversity, and inclusion in education. Educational leaders are increasingly focused on addressing disparities in educational outcomes based on factors such as race, ethnicity, socio-economic status, gender, and ability. They are working to create inclusive learning environments that promote access, opportunity, and success for all students.

Collaborative Leadership: Educational leadership is becoming more collaborative and distributed, emphasizing shared decision-making and teamwork among administrators, teachers, parents, and community stakeholders. Leaders are fostering collaborative cultures within schools and districts, promoting communication, trust, and collective problem-solving (Carney et al., 2015).

Data-Informed Decision Making: With the proliferation of data and assessment tools, educational leaders are increasingly using data to inform decision-making and drive school improvement efforts. They are analyzing student performance data, identifying trends and patterns, and using evidence-based practices to support teaching and learning (Barnes et al., 2019). Technological Integration: Technology is playing an increasingly important role in education, transforming teaching and learning experiences. Educational leaders are leveraging technology to enhance instruction, personalize learning, and expand access to educational resources. They are implementing technology integration initiatives, providing professional development for teachers, and ensuring equitable access to digital tools and resources.

Focus on 21st Century Skills: Educational leadership is shifting towards a focus on 21st-century skills, such as critical thinking, communication, collaboration, creativity, and digital literacy. Leaders are working to align curriculum and instruction with the demands of the modern workforce, preparing students to thrive in an increasingly complex and interconnected world.

Culturally Responsive Leadership: Educational leaders are adopting culturally responsive practices that recognize and value students' diverse cultural backgrounds and experiences. They are promoting culturally relevant curriculum, providing professional development on cultural competence, and fostering inclusive school climates that celebrate diversity (Demirtas & Karaca, 2020).

Adaptive Leadership: In response to rapid change and uncertainty, educational leaders are adopting adaptive leadership approaches that emphasize flexibility, resilience, and innovation. They are adept at navigating complex challenges, fostering a culture of continuous learning and improvement, and leading change initiatives that promote organizational agility and sustainability.

These shifts and trends in educational leadership reflect a dynamic and evolving landscape, as leaders strive to meet the diverse needs of students, families, and communities in the 21st century. By embracing these changes and staying abreast of emerging research and best practices, educational leaders can effectively lead their organizations towards success and excellence.

Traditional leadership models in education have long been the cornerstone of organizational structures within academic establishments. These models have traditionally emphasised hierarchical systems, top-down decision-making procedures, and a focal point on keeping the fame quo. Leaders in these traditional models were regularly seen as authoritative figures who directed and managed these moves within the organization. However, because the panorama of education continues to adapt, there's a growing popularity of the limitations of those traditional leadership models. The increasing number of complex challenges facing educational establishments require a dynamic and adaptable leadership technique. In response to this need, new perspectives on transformative leadership have emerged, hard the conventional notions of leadership in education. By exploring tutorial leadership's historical evolution, we can gain valuable insights into the factors that have shaped our modern knowledge of leadership in education. This journey through the beyond can provide a foundation for knowledge of the shifts that have taken place and the motives in the back of the emergence of recent views on transformative leadership (Cojocaru, 2023).

As we delve into the historical context of educational leadership, we can discover the numerous influences which have model leadership practices over time. From the early days of education systems to the cutting edge, there have been extensive adjustments within the way leadership is conceptualized and enacted within educational settings. By examining those changes, we will begin to respect the complexities of leadership in education and the want for a more inclusive and collaborative method. In the subsequent sections, explore the important thing milestones in the historical evolution of educational leadership, highlighting the shifts in thinking and practice. By understanding the historical context of leadership in education, we can better respect the significance of embracing new perspectives and approaches that are highly ideal for addressing the demanding situations of the 21st century.

2.1   Traditional Leadership Models

As we delve into the ancient evolution of educational leadership, it is imperative to shed light on the traditional leadership models which have shaped the landscape of academia. These model have played a big role in defining the function of leaders within educational establishments and feature had an enduring effect on the way leadership is perceived and practised within the area of education.

Autocratic Leadership

One of the maximum frequent traditional leadership models in education is autocratic leadership. In this model, the leader holds all of the energy and decision-making authority, with little to no entry from subordinates. Decisions are rendered independently, and there exists a distinct pecking order within the organization. While this style of leadership can be effective in situations that require brief decision-making and a clear chain of command, it can additionally stifle creativity and innovation amongst a group of workers contributors.

Bureaucratic Leadership

Bureaucratic leadership is any other traditional model that has been widely followed in educational settings. In this model, leaders adhere strictly to regulations, policies, and approaches, often at the expense of flexibility and adaptability. Decisions are made based totally on mounted protocols, and there may be an emphasis on maintaining order and balance in the business enterprise. While this approach may be effective in ensuring consistency and responsibility, it may additionally restrict progress and innovation.

Transactional Leadership

Transactional leadership is a conventional model that focuses on alternate rewards and punishments to motivate followers. Leaders set clear expectancies and goals for his or her subordinates and offer rewards for meeting or exceeding these expectancies, at the same time as additionally imposing effects for failing to accomplish that. While this model can be effective in promoting duty and attaining quick-term desires, it may not be conducive to fostering long-term growth and development among staff members (Collins, 2017).

Charismatic Leadership

Charismatic leadership is a traditional model that centres around the personality and charisma of the leader. Charismatic leaders are frequently visible as inspirational figures who can encourage and impact others through their imaginative and prescient ardour. While this approach may be powerful in rallying aid and growing a feeling of unity within an organization, it could also lead to dependency on the leader and a lack of focus on institutional goals and objectives.

Transformational Leadership

While traditional leadership models have performed an extensive role in shaping educational leadership practices, there has been a shift towards greater present-day approaches such as transformational leadership. Transformational leaders encourage and empower their followers to attain better performance and personal growth by fostering a shared vision, promoting innovation, and inspiring a collaborative and supportive environment. This method emphasizes the significance of constructing robust relationships, growing the ability of workforce individuals, and creating a culture of continuous improvement.

Distributed Leadership

Distributed leadership is a modern technique of leadership that emphasizes the sharing of obligations and decision-making among diverse individuals within an employer. This model is based totally on the concept that leadership isn't constrained to single persons on the pinnacle of a hierarchy, but as an alternative can be disbursed at some stage in the employer (Caban-Martinez et al., 2022). By establishing connections with numerous stakeholders throughout the leadership process, distributed leadership can foster collaboration, stimulate innovation, and cultivate a communal perception of ownership of the organization's goals and objectives. This technique contrasts with greater traditional types of leadership, which often centre around a single leader who holds most of the power and authority.

Autocratic Leadership in Education: A Traditional Leadership Model

Autocratic leadership, a dominant style in conventional educational leadership style, is characterised by a top-down technique where the leader holds absolute strength and makes decisions without tons of input from others. This style of leadership is deeply rooted in the historic evolution of educational leadership and has been both praised for its performance and criticized for its loss of inclusivity and collaboration. Autocratic leadership in education may be traced returned to the early days of formal training whilst authority figures which included headmasters and principals were expected to possess whole manage over the educational group (Hartati & Muktar, 2019). This hierarchical structure became believed to hold subject and order in the education setting, making sure that students followed regulations and regulations set with followed rules and regulations set by the leader. In the 20th century, at some point in intervals of industrialization and standardization in education, autocratic leadership became in addition reinforced as a means to streamline processes and obtain uniformity in teaching strategies and curriculum delivery. Leaders have been regularly visible because the closing decision-makers, with little room for deviation from their directives.

Characteristics of Autocratic Leadership

Centralized Decision-Making: In the realm of autocratic leadership, determinations are exclusively rendered by the leader, devoid of any inclination to solicit input or feedback from educators or other invested parties. This can lead to quick decision-making but may overlook valuable perspectives and ideas.

Strict Control: Leaders exert strict authority over all facets of the educational establishment, encompassing the orchestration of academic syllabi, allocation of resources, and implementation of disciplinary measures. This can create a sense of rigidity and conformity within the organization.

Limited Communication: Communication flows primarily from the leader to subordinates, with little opportunity for open dialogue or discussion. This can hinder creativity and innovation among educators and staff members.

Hierarchical Structure: Autocratic leadership often reinforces a strict hierarchy within the organization, with clear lines of authority and little room for autonomy or empowerment among lower-level staff. Autocratic leadership, despite its potential benefits in specific circumstances, such as urgent decision-making during crises, can also present notable disadvantages in an educational environment. Some of the impacts of autocratic leadership in education include:

Limited Professional Growth: Educators and teams of workers may additionally experience disempowered and undervalued, main to reduced process pride and motivation. This can hinder professional development and growth within the organization (Abraham et al., 2021).

Lack of Innovation: Autocratic leadership can inhibit innovation and experimentation in teaching methods and curriculum design by stifling creativity and independent thinking. This can result in a stagnant educational environment that fails to adapt to changing needs and trends.

Poor Stakeholder Engagement: When leaders fail to involve stakeholders in decision-making procedures, they hazard alienating educators, students, parents, and the network at massive. This can result in a loss of agreement and collaboration inside the educational group.

As the field of education continues to adapt, there may be a growing recognition of the restrictions of autocratic leadership in fostering a dynamic and inclusive mastering environment. Many educational leaders at the moment are embracing more participatory and collaborative tactics that emphasize shared decision-making, open communication, and empowerment of stakeholders. By transitioning far away from conventional autocratic models towards transformative leadership styles, educators can domesticate a subculture of acceptance as true with, collaboration, and innovation that meets the numerous desires of ultra-modern freshmen. This shift toward an extra-inclusive and empowering leadership paradigm holds the capacity to transform education and create more equitable and engaging experiences for all (Aagaard & Earnest, 2021).

Bureaucratic Leadership in Education: A Traditional Leadership Model

The concept of bureaucratic leadership has been widely regarded as a traditional and fundamental framework. Stemming from the theories posited by Max Weber during the initial years of the twentieth century, bureaucratic leadership places significant emphasis on explicit hierarchies, clearly defined roles and responsibilities, and strict adherence to established regulations and methodologies. Within the realm of education, bureaucratic leadership has found extensive application in schools, schools, and other academic establishments to ensure efficacy, responsibility, and organisational equilibrium.

One of the key traits of bureaucratic leadership in education is its emphasis on formal authority and a top-down decision-making structure. School administrators, principals, and other leaders are anticipated to make decisions based on set-up policies and regulations as opposed to personal preferences or individual discretion. This hierarchical technique of leadership is meant to promote consistency, fairness, and uniformity in academic practices and policies. Moreover, bureaucratic leadership in education often involves a high diploma of specialisation and department of labour. Different roles and obligations are genuinely described, with each member of the company anticipated to fulfil their unique responsibilities in the installed framework. This division of labour enables to ensure that obligations are completed successfully and efficaciously, contributing to the general functioning of the educational institution (Abdi et al., 2022).

Another hallmark of bureaucratic leadership in education is its reliance on formalised conversation channels and documentation. Decisions, guidelines, and techniques are commonly communicated through respectable channels, consisting of memos, conferences, and respectable files, to ensure clarity and transparency. Additionally, bureaucratic leaders in education frequently keep special statistics and documentation to track progress, examine performance, and make certain compliance with guidelines. While bureaucratic leadership has performed a significant role in shaping academic institutions for many years, it isn't without its boundaries and criticisms. Critics of bureaucratic leadership argue that its emphasis on guidelines and techniques can stifle innovation, creativity, and flexibility in educational settings. The rigid hierarchies and centralized decision-making methods may additionally preclude collaboration, conversation, and flexibility in response to converting educational desires and challenges.

In examining the historical evolution of educational leadership, it's miles critical to recollect the position of bureaucratic leadership in the academic context. Bureaucratic leadership represents a traditional model of leadership that has had a big impact on educational institutions. This leadership style is characterised by clear hierarchies, formal policies and tactics, and a focus on performance and compliance. In the sphere of education, bureaucratic leadership has regularly been associated with centralized decision-making, standardized processes, and a top-down technique to control. Despite its conventional nature, bureaucratic leadership has fundamentally shaped educational structures around the sector (Adams, 2018). It has provided stability, consistency, and structure to educational organisations, assisting in making sure that they run smoothly and efficiently. Bureaucratic leaders in education are commonly responsible for setting clear goals and expectancies, organising regulations and strategies, and overseeing the everyday operations of schools and educational institutions.

While bureaucratic leadership has its benefits in terms of organizational efficiency and balance, it additionally has its boundaries. Critics argue that this leadership style can be rigid, inflexible, and slow to adapt to trade. In the modern-day unexpectedly evolving educational landscape, where innovation and creativity are increasingly valued, bureaucratic leadership may also war to maintain pace with the needs of the 21st century.

Key Features of Bureaucratic Leadership

Hierarchical Structure: Bureaucratic leadership is characterized by a clear chain of command, with authority flowing from the pinnacle down. Decisions are made by the ones in positions of authority, and subordinates are anticipated to observe instructions without query.

Standardized Procedures: Bureaucratic groups depend on standardized approaches to make certain consistency and predictability in operations. Rules and regulations govern each factor of the organisation, from decision-making to everyday obligations.

Focus on Rules and Regulations: Bureaucratic leaders adhere strictly to established rules and regulations. They prioritize compliance with guidelines and tactics, frequently at the price of flexibility and innovation.

Impersonal Relationships: In a bureaucratic setting, relationships between leaders and followers are often impersonal. Decisions are based totally on objective standards in preference to personal decisions or emotions.

In the context of education, bureaucratic leadership has been praised and criticized for its leadership can help preserve order and consistency in educational establishments. By following mounted regulations and regulations, school leaders can ensure that policies are implemented uniformly and fairly. However, critics of bureaucratic leadership in education factor to its ability drawbacks. The rigid adherence to guidelines and policies can stifle creativity and innovation in schools. Educators and administrators may also feel limited by using bureaucratic red tape, leading to a lack of autonomy and initiative in decision-making (Aiston et al., 2020).

As the ever-evolving terrain of education persists, leaders are faced with the formidable task of harmonizing the advantages of bureaucratic leadership with the desire for pliability and adjustability. In a trendy rapidly changing world, schools need to be able to reply quickly to new challenges and opportunities. The bureaucratic style of leadership, characterized by its ardent focus on established regulations and procedures, may not invariably align with the inherently changeable and ever-evolving essence of contemporary education. To cope with these demanding situations, educational leaders are more and more turning to transformative leadership strategies that emphasize collaboration, innovation, and continuous improvement. By fostering a way of life of agreeing with, transparency, and shared imaginative and prescient, transformative leaders can inspire positive change and drive meaningful progress in education. By combining the best elements of traditional leadership models with progressive practices, educational leaders can create an extra inclusive, dynamic, and transformative knowledge of the environment for all.

Transactional Leadership in Traditional Educational Leadership Models

Transactional Leadership, as a leadership style, is predicated solely upon a transactional dynamic or reciprocal agreement established between the leader and their followers. This model operates on the idea that followers are influenced through a device of rewards and punishments. In the context of education, this style of leadership was time-honoured in the conventional school structures wherein hierarchical systems and authority had been the norm. In the domain of educational administration, transactional leadership stands as one of the traditional leadership styles that has received extensive scholarly attention and implementation (Collins, 2017). This paradigm, defined by the act of exchanging rewards and punishments in response to performance, has exerted a considerable influence on the academic domain over time. In conventional educational settings, Transactional Leadership turned into often the predominant style of leadership appointed by school administrators and educators. The hierarchical shape of the school, with clear lines of authority and guidelines to be followed, lent itself properly to this model of leadership. Educators might set clear expectations for school students in phrases of educational performance, behaviour and participation. Students who met those expectations were rewarded with suitable grades, rewards or other styles of recognition. On the opposite hand, school students who did not meet the standards confronted results along with detention, lower grades or even suspension. Administrators might frequently practice leadership through exception, intervening simplest while there had been disciplinary issues or academic problems that needed to be addressed. This reactive approach to leadership helped maintain order and discipline within the school environmen (Al-Mansoori & Koç, 2019)t.

To apprehend the results and applications of transactional leadership in education, it's far critical to delve into its historic evolution and explore its various components. Transactional leadership strains its roots back to the early 20th century whilst industrialization and the need for organizational performance brought about the emergence of leadership theories targeted at task-oriented leadership. In the sphere of education, transactional leadership garnered significant attention during the middle of the 20th century, as educational establishments and schools began to embrace more organized and hierarchical approaches to leadership. During this period, educational leaders relied on transactional strategies to maintain order, implement regulations, and ensure compliance among students and personnel. The transactional model operated based on a clear chain of command, with leaders setting particular goals and expectations and using rewards and punishments to incentivize performance and area.

Key Features of Transactional Leadership

Contingent Reward

At the centre of transactional leadership in education is the concept of contingent praise, wherein leaders establish clear expectancies and goals for their subordinates and provide rewards or popularity for assembly or exceeding those expectations. This element of transactional leadership is based on the standards of reinforcement concept, in which fantastic effects are linked to desired behaviours. Educational leaders who hire contingent reward mechanisms often use incentives which include praise, popularity, grades or other varieties of acknowledgement to encourage school students and staff to attain educational or organizational goals. By setting up a clear link between overall performance and rewards, leaders can create a structured and purpose-orientated environment that fosters duty and productivity (Jiang et al., 2023).

Leadership by Exception

Another crucial element of transactional leadership in the field of education is the implementation of leadership by exception, whereby the establishment of well-defined boundaries and criteria for satisfactory achievement is accompanied by intervention solely in instances of deviation. In this particular strategy, leaders are responsible for establishing regulations, guidelines, and protocols which precisely outline the permissible boundaries of conduct and achievement. Consequently, leaders solely intercede or execute corrective measures when these pre-established benchmarks are not attained. Transactional leaders who employ leadership by exception strategies focus on monitoring and controlling outcomes, addressing issues as they arise, and ensuring compliance with established norms and guidelines. By maintaining a vigilant stance and responding to deviations promptly, leaders can uphold order and discipline within educational settings (Al-Moamary et al., 2020).

Passive Leadership by Exception

In contrast to active leadership by exception, passive leadership by exception involves a more hands-off approach to leadership, where leaders intervene only when problems escalate or performance deteriorates significantly. This reactive style of transactional leadership relies on the assumption that individuals will self-regulate and meet expectations without constant oversight, and leaders only step in when issues become critical.

Educational leaders who adopt passive leadership by exception may delegate responsibilities to subordinates, provide minimal guidance or support, and intervene only when problems reach a critical threshold. While this technique can promote autonomy and independence among students and the body of workers, it could additionally result in troubles being ignored or neglected until they reach a disaster point.

While transactional leadership has its merits in terms of retaining order and ensuring compliance, it additionally has its boundaries. Critics argue that this style of leadership can stifle creativity, innovation, and intrinsic motivation among school students. By focusing entirely on external rewards and punishments, leaders may additionally fail to faucet into the intrinsic motivations of school students to learn and grow. Moreover, transactional leadership can create a tradition of dependency on outside rewards, where students emerge as more centred on achieving rewards rather than on the learning process itself. This can lead to a narrow awareness of extrinsic consequences together with grades, at the price of broader academic goals which include essential thinking, creativity, and problem-solving abilities (Smith & McPherson, 2020).

Charismatic Leadership in Traditional Educational Leadership Models

Amidst the conventional paradigms of educational leadership, charismatic leadership emerged as a disruptive pressure that challenged conventional notions of authority and influence. Coined by Max Weber, charismatic leadership is characterised by way of the chief's capacity to encourage and encourage followers through their aura and vision. This particular form of leadership is distinguished by the leader's capability to stimulate and influence others using their charisma and foresight. Leaders of a charismatic nature are often regarded as visionary and motivational individuals who exert a deep influence on those who follow them. The roots of charismatic leadership may be traced back to historical instances, with charismatic leaders including Alexander the Great and Julius Caesar fascinating their followers with their charisma and their charisma and vision. In the realm of education, the manifestation of charismatic leadership has been epitomized through the utilization of notable individuals such as Maria Montessori and Paulo Freire, who invigorated numerous cohorts of educators with their innovative methods of instruction and acquisition. Charismatic leaders are acknowledged for their aptitude in articulating a compelling aspiration for the forthcoming and inspiring others to unite in support of said aspiration. They possess a sturdy feel of purpose and might talk about their goals and values in a manner that resonates with their followers. This potential to encourage and encourage others is a key thing of charismatic leadership and sets it other from more traditional types of leadership.

The historical evolution of educational leadership has witnessed the emergence of charismatic leadership as a transformative force within traditional models. By challenging established norms and inspiring followers through vision and charisma, charismatic leaders have the potential to revolutionize educational practices and drive meaningful change. As educational establishments navigate the complexities of the modern international, embracing the ideas of charismatic leadership can pave the way for a more dynamic and inclusive approach to leadership in education.

Key Characteristics of Charismatic Leadership

Visionary Leadership: Charismatic leaders are recognised for his or her ability to articulate a compelling imaginative and prescient that resonates with followers. By creating a brilliant image of a higher future, they inspire others to rally at the back of their motive and paintings towards a not-unusual intention (Galli et al., 2017).

Emotional Intelligence: Charismatic leaders possess an excessive degree of emotional intelligence, permitting them to connect with individuals on a personal stage. This empathetic technique fosters agreement with and loyalty among followers, growing a sense of camaraderie and shared cause.

Transformational Influence: Through their charismatic presence and persuasive communication style, charismatic leaders have the power to effect profound transformations within organizations. They challenge the status quo, ignite innovation, and drive change through their infectious enthusiasm and unwavering conviction.

Charismatic Authority: Unlike traditional leaders who derive authority from formal positions, charismatic leaders wield authority based totally on their traits and the emotional connection they set up with their followers. This shape of authority is dynamic and contingent on the chief's potential to encourage and interact with others.

While this leadership style has its strengths, it's miles essential for educational leaders to recall its barriers and to discover alternative methods, together with transformative leadership, which can provide a greater sustainable and inclusive model for leading academic institutions into their future. By significantly inspecting the historic evolution of educational leadership and the role of charismatic leadership in this context, educators can benefit from new views on a way to efficiently lead and encourage others in a hastily changing educational landscape. One of the key strengths of charismatic leadership is its ability to engender enthusiasm and commitment among followers. Charismatic leaders are adept at fostering a sense of shared cause and identity amongst their followers, which could result in improved motivation and engagement. This may be especially treasured in academic settings, in which inspiring and tasty school students and educators are essential to fostering a tremendous learning environment. However, charismatic leadership is not without its obstacles. One capability disadvantage of this leadership style is its reliance on the persona and aura of the leader. Charismatic leaders might also battle to maintain their impact if they are unable to maintain the initial exhilaration and exuberance that attracted followers in the first vicinity. Additionally, charismatic leaders may be perceived as overly dominant or authoritarian, which can undermine collaboration and teamwork in an enterprise (Azimirad et al., 2022).

Transformational Leadership in Traditional Educational Leadership Models

In contrast to traditional leadership models, transformational leadership emerged as a reaction to the limitations of hierarchical structures and authoritarian leadership patterns. Coined via James MacGregor Burns in the Nineteen Seventies, transformational leadership emphasizes the significance of inspiring and motivating followers to obtain collective desires, tough the reputation quo, and promote non-stop growth and improvement. Transformational leaders are visionaries who articulate a compelling vision for the future of the employer, encourage others to proportion in that vision, and empower individuals to contribute their particular capabilities and perspectives toward its consciousness. By fostering a culture of collaboration, creativity, and shared decision-making, transformational leaders create an experience of ownership and funding among stakeholders, main to accelerated engagement, motivation, and performance. Moreover, transformational leadership places a robust emphasis on individualized consideration, intellectual stimulation, and idealized impact as key additives of powerful leadership. By spotting and valuing the contributions of every team member, encouraging crucial thinking and innovation, and modelling ethical behaviour and integrity, transformational leaders cultivate a positive organizational weather that promotes increase, learning, and achievement (Corlett & McConnachie, 2021).

To certainly apprehend the importance of transformational leadership within the context of traditional leadership style in education, it's miles essential to delve into the historical evolution of educational leadership. In the early days, educational leadership was often characterized using a top-down technique, where decision-making and authority were centralized at the pinnacle of the hierarchy. This conventional model of leadership emphasised leadership, compliance, and efficiency, with leaders predicted to oversee and manage the everyday operations of educational institutions. Transformational leadership represents a departure from the conventional authoritarian style of leadership, focusing on a substitute for inspiring and empowering followers to obtain better stages of overall performance and personal growth. In the middle of transformational leadership are four key components: idealized influence, inspirational motivation, intellectual stimulation, and individualized consideration.

Idealized Influence: Transformational leaders lead by way of example, demonstrating integrity, credibility, and a strong feel of motive. They serve as function model for his or her followers, earning their recognition and admiration.

Inspirational Motivation: Transformational leaders encourage and motivate their followers with the aid of articulating a compelling imaginative and prescient and tough them to attain their full capability. They communicate high expectations and foster a sense of collective purpose and commitment.

Intellectual Stimulation: Transformational leaders function as a supply of inspiration, motivating their followers to enhance their creativity foster innovation, and interact in important thinking. They challenge the status quo, promote continuous learning, and empower individuals to think independently and solve problems collaboratively.

Individualized Consideration: Transformational leaders demonstrate an authentic challenge for the well-being and development of each character within their group. They provide personalised aid, teaching, and comments to help individuals grow and thrive.

Integrating Transformational Leadership within Traditional Models

While transformational leadership represents a paradigm shift from conventional authoritarian styles, it is crucial to recognize that factors of both strategies can coexist within educational leadership practices. Rather than viewing transformational leadership as a wholesale alternative to traditional models, academic leaders can leverage its concepts to beautify and complement existing structures and procedures. One way to integrate transformational leadership within conventional styles is to undertake a dispensed leadership method, wherein leadership responsibilities are shared amongst multiple stakeholders, inclusive of educators, directors, school students, and parents. By decentralizing decision-making authority and empowering individuals in any respect tiers of the agency, schools can tap right into a numerous range of views, understanding, and thoughts, leading to extra revolutionary and effective answers to complex challenges. Additionally, educational leaders can domesticate a transformational leadership mindset by actively seeking remarks, fostering a lifestyle of continuous improvement, and investing in professional development possibilities for a team of workers. By prioritizing collaboration, conversation, and mentorship, leaders can create supportive and inclusive surroundings in which all individuals in the school network sense valued, respected, and empowered to contribute to their excellence (Fekadu et al., 2021).

Distributed Leadership in Traditional Leadership Models

Distributed leadership is a present-day method that emphasizes the shared duty and collaborative nature of leadership in an organisation. Distributed leadership is based totally on the premise that powerful leadership isn't always the only duty of one character but is a collective endeavour that entails the whole school network. In a dispensed leadership model, leadership duties are shared amongst educators, administrators, school students, parents, and other participants of the school network. This approach recognizes that every stakeholder brings unique strengths, understanding, and perspectives to the desk and that via operating together collaboratively, they can gain higher consequences for the school. Distributed leadership isn't always approximately delegating responsibilities or diluting authority, but rather about harnessing the collective intelligence and creativity of the entire network to power continuous improvement and innovation.

To apprehend the concept of distributed leadership in conventional styles, it's miles essential to delve into the historical evolution of educational leadership. Historically, educational leadership was regularly characterised by using hierarchical systems, wherein authority and decision-making were concentrated at the top of the organizational hierarchy.

This conventional model of leadership became primarily based on the perception that a single individual, normally the most important or head instructor, became answerable for making all important decisions and placing the route for the school (Akin et al., 2023). Within the traditional model of educational leadership, disbursed leadership can tackle various forms. One commonplace approach is for the foremost or head instructor to delegate precise leadership duties to different members of the school network. For example, an instructor may be tasked with main a curriculum development crew, while a parent can be chargeable for organizing a school occasion. Another manner in which disbursed leadership can take place within the conventional model is through the established order of leadership teams or committees. These teams bring collectively representatives from unique stakeholder organizations to collaborate on key decision-making processes, consisting of strategic planning, budgeting, and coverage improvement. In a few instances, allotted leadership inside the conventional model may additionally involve the promotion of teacher leadership. This can take the form of instructor-led projects, including professional studying groups or action research projects, wherein educators take on leadership roles in driving school improvement efforts.

Key Characteristics of Distributed Leadership

Shared Leadership: In a distributed leadership model, leadership obligations are shared among diverse stakeholders, with every playing a position in shaping the vision, desires, and route of the corporation. This shared approach to leadership fosters an experience of possession, accountability, and dedication among all individuals in the educational community.

Collaborative Decision-Making: Distributed leadership emphasizes collaborative decision-making tactics, wherein stakeholders work together to pick out challenges, explore solutions, and make knowledgeable decisions which are in the exceptional hobby of students and the overall school network. By considering a couple of perspectives within the decision-making procedure, allotted leadership can result in extra modern and effective answers to complex troubles.

Professional Learning Communities: A key issue of distributed leadership is the advent of experts gaining knowledge of communities, in which educators and other stakeholders have the opportunity to collaborate, replicate exercises, share resources, and interact in continuous studying and improvement. These communities offer a platform for ongoing communication, collaboration, and expert increase, which are vital for building a subculture of non-stop development in educational establishments (Asakawa et al., 2017). There are several benefits to implementing distributed leadership within conventional models of educational leadership. One of the important thing advantages is that it promotes a more inclusive and democratic decision-making procedure, in which a couple of voices and perspectives are heard. Furthermore, distributed leadership can help to build a sense of possession and duty amongst all individuals of the school community, main to accelerated motivation and commitment to reaching shared goals. By distributed leadership duties, schools can also faucet into a much wider variety of understanding and competencies, leading to extra progressive and effective solutions to complex challenges.

2.2   Shifts and Trends in Educational Leadership

By knowing the historic evolution of educational leadership and the shifts and traits that have formed the sector, educators can develop new perspectives on transformative leadership in education. Embracing collaboration, visionary leadership, distributed leadership, transformational leadership and proactive leadership can help educational leaders navigate the complexities of cutting-edge education structures and force effective change for school students, educators, and groups alike. The Industrial Revolution brought about huge modifications in educational leadership because the need for skilled employees and a standardized curriculum became paramount. Educational leaders at some point in this period centred on performance and duty, searching to prepare students for the demands of the emerging industrial society (Herbst, 2020).

Shifts and Trends in Educational Leadership

From Authority to Collaboration: One of the key shifts in educational leadership has been the flow from a pinnacle-down, authoritarian model to a greater collaborative and inclusive technique. Modern academic leaders are expected to work collaboratively with educators, parents, and community members to create a shared vision and mission for the school.

From Leadership to Visionary Leadership: While administrative and managerial skills are nonetheless important in educational leadership, there was a growing emphasis on visionary leadership that inspires and motivates others closer to a common goal. Visionary education leaders can assume strategically, innovate, and adapt to converting circumstances.

From Individual to Distributed Leadership: Another trend in educational leadership is the move toward allotted leadership, wherein leadership duties are shared among more than one stakeholder in the school community. This technique recognizes that leadership can and need to come from diverse sources, consisting of educators, school students, and parents (Boche, 2022).

From Transactional to Transformational Leadership: Traditional transactional leadership which focuses on rewarding performance and implementing policies, has given way to transformational leadership in education. Transformational leaders inspire and empower others to gain their full capability, fostering a culture of growth, innovation, and continuous improvement.

From Reactive to Proactive Leadership: In today's rapidly changing academic landscape, proactive leadership has become vital. Educational leaders should expect and reply to rising challenges and possibilities, instead of surely reacting to them. Proactive leaders are strategic, ahead-questioning, forward-thinking, and agile in their decision-making.

From Authority to Collaboration: Shifts and Trends in Educational Leadership

The shift from authority to collaboration in academic leadership represents a fundamental exchange in how we technique leadership within the subject of education. By embracing a greater collaborative and inclusive model of leadership, educational leaders can empower their teams, build strong partnerships, and create a way of life of belief and innovation. This new perspective on transformative leadership in education holds the potential to pressure high-quality change and enhance effects for school students, educators, and communities alike. From traditional authoritative models to greater collaborative and inclusive techniques, the historic evolution of educational leadership reflects broader societal shifts and developments within the discipline (Anderson & Heenan, 2021). One of the important things transitions in educational leadership is the shift from authority-based models to collaborative ones, marking a vast departure from top-down decision-making to greater participatory and empowering practices. The shift from authority to collaboration reflects a broader reputation of the importance of distributed leadership, shared decision-making, and participatory strategies in driving advantageous alternatives in educational settings. This evolution is motivated by different factors, which include converting social norms, advances in the era, and a developing emphasis on inclusivity and diversity.

Shared Decision-Making: One of the important thing aspects of the move toward collaborative leadership is the emphasis on shared decision-making approaches. Rather than decisions being made unilaterally using a single authority figure, collaborative leaders engage with stakeholders at all levels to gather enter, remarks, and perspectives. This inclusive approach now not only leads to greater knowledge and effective decisions but also fosters a feeling of ownership and buy-in among team members.

Empowerment and Trust: Collaborative leadership is also characterized by a focal point of empowerment and consideration. Leaders who undertake a collaborative approach empower their group individuals to take possession of their work, make self-reliant decisions, and make contributions of their particular talents and knowledge to the collective effort. This culture of belief and empowerment creates a nice and supportive work environment where individuals are inspired to excel and innovate (Abel et al., 2020).

Building Networks and Partnerships: In the collaborative leadership model, educational leaders apprehend the value of constructing networks and partnerships both inside and outside their corporations. By forging connections with other educational institutions, network corporations, and stakeholders, leaders can leverage collective resources, proportion pleasant practices, and work closer to commonplace goals. This collaborative community technique permits leaders to tap into a wealth of knowledge and learning, driving innovation and continuous development in education.

Promoting Diversity and Inclusivity: Another important aspect of collaborative leadership is the promotion of diversity and inclusivity. By actively seeking out numerous perspectives, backgrounds, and stories, leaders can create an extra inclusive and equitable academic environment. This commitment to range no longer handiest enriches the learning revel for school students however also fosters a lifestyle of recognition, empathy, and understanding among all contributors to the educational network.

From Leadership to Visionary Leadership: Shifts and Trends in Educational Leadership

The shift from leadership to visionary leadership in education represents an essential evolution within the academic leader's technique of their roles and responsibilities. Visionary leadership is characterized by using a focal point on inspiring and motivating stakeholders closer to a shared vision of educational excellence. Instead of handling daily operations, visionary leaders are proactive in shaping the future route in their institutions and driving innovation and exchange. Visionary leaders can create vibrant learning groups that inspire excellence and innovation by embracing collaboration, continuous improvement, and a focus on student-focused methods. As the sphere of educational leadership continues to conform, leaders need to conform to these new perspectives and tendencies to effectively meet the demanding situations of the 21st-century educational landscape. This evolution has been prompted using various historical tendencies that have formed the landscape of educational leadership through the years. Leaders have been visible as managers whose primary position turned to maintaining order and efficiency within the corporation. This leadership-centric method has persisted for many years, with leaders being evaluated based totally on their potential to manage resources, allocate budgets, and enforce guidelines. It has become increasingly clear that academic leaders had to adopt a more transformative and visionary stance to effectively navigate the challenges of the contemporary educational panorama (Al-Zboon, 2016).

One of the important aspects of visionary leadership is the emphasis on collaboration and shared decision-making. Instead of top-down directives, visionary leaders interact with educators, students, parents, and community participants to co-create an imaginative and prescient for the future of the institution. This collaborative technique no longer best fosters an experience of possession and buy-in among stakeholders however also ensures that the vision is aligned with the needs and aspirations of the entire school community. Another hallmark of visionary leadership is a robust recognition of continuous improvement and expert development. Visionary leaders are dedicated to developing a way of life of getting to know their establishments, wherein educators are endorsed to test, take risks, and develop professionally. By investing in the increase and development of their team of workers, visionary leaders can domesticate a way of life of excellence and innovation that permeates every aspect of the group (Frykedal et al., 2016).

Several key shifts and trends have inspired the evolution toward visionary leadership in education. One of the most significant developments is the growing emphasis on student-focused processes for teaching and learning. As educators have moved far away from conventional, one-length-suits-all academic strategies, there has been a corresponding shift closer to leadership that prioritizes individualized learning stories and the holistic development of students. Another important trend is the developing recognition of the significance of social and emotional knowledge in education. Visionary leaders understand that educational fulfilment is the best factor in a student's growth and development and region a strong emphasis on cultivating social and emotional abilities inclusive of empathy, resilience, and self-attention. By fostering supportive and nurturing surroundings that address the holistic needs of school students, visionary leaders can create a way of life of inclusivity and belonging within their institutions.

From Individual to Distributed Leadership: Shifts and Trends in Educational Leadership
The shift from character to distributed leadership in education represents a large evolution in how leadership is conceptualized and practised inside educational institutions. By embracing shared leadership, collaboration, and collective decision-making, educational leaders can harness numerous stakeholders' skills, views, and understanding to force meaningful and sustainable growth within schools and districts. As the sphere of educational leadership continues to adapt, the adoption of a distributed leadership model can assist in building extra resilient, responsive, and progressive educational corporations which are highly geared up to satisfy the complex demanding situations of the 21st century (Al Issa & Abdelsalam, 2021).

One of the key shifts in educational leadership is the pass from individual leadership to distributed leadership, an idea that emphasizes shared responsibilities, collaboration, and collective decision-making amongst diverse stakeholders inside the educational community. Distributed leadership is based on the idea that leadership isn't always the only obligation of one person however is instead a shared and collective endeavour that includes the lively participation and collaboration of more than one stakeholder, which includes educators, directors, students, parents and network individuals. Under the distributed leadership model, leadership duties are distributed throughout numerous people and corporations within the organization, with every stakeholder contributing their particular skills, understanding, and views to the decision-making technique. This collaborative approach to leadership is grounded in the notion that the collective information and information of the entire academic community are critical for using significant and sustainable growth in schools and districts.

The shift towards distributed leadership in education reflects broader trends and shifts in the field of educational leadership, including:

Emphasis on Collaboration and Teamwork: In the modern day rapidly changing educational landscape, the need for collaboration, teamwork, and collective problem-solving has end up increasingly essential. Distributed leadership aligns with this trend with the aid of emphasizing the value of shared leadership and collaborative decision-making procedures.

Recognition of Diverse Perspectives and Expertise: As schools and districts emerge as greater numerous and complex, the recognition of numerous perspectives and expertise in the educational network has emerged as crucial for using innovation and development. Distributed leadership allows for the inclusion of more than one voice and viewpoint in the decision-making system, which can result in extra knowledgeable and powerful techniques and answers.

Focus on Empowerment and Agency: Distributed leadership empowers people within the academic network to take on leadership roles, share their know-how and contribute to the collective achievement of the agency. This cognizance of empowerment and enterprise promotes a sense of ownership, autonomy, and engagement among stakeholders, which are crucial for fostering a culture of continuous improvement and innovation.

From Transactional to Transformational Leadership: Shifts and Trends in Educational Leadership

In educational leadership, the evolution of leadership patterns has seen a widespread shift from transactional to transformational methods. The shift from transactional to transformational leadership in education displays a broader trend toward extra collaborative, inspiring, and student-centred techniques in leadership (Al-Zboon, 2016). By embracing the ideas of transformational leadership, educational leaders can create significant and impactful growth within their school, driving innovation, growth, and fulfilment for all members of the school community. These shifts and tendencies have paved the way for an extra dynamic and effective form of leadership in educational institutions. Transformational leaders seek to create an extremely good and engaging learning environment that fosters student increase and fulfilment. They prioritize constructing sturdy relationships with educators, college students, and parents and are devoted to continuous development and innovation in teaching and learning practices. The shift from transactional to transformational leadership in education has been influenced by way of numerous key shifts and developments in the subject of educational leadership.

Focus on Student-Centered Learning: With a growing emphasis on individualized learning and student-centric methodologies, educational officials are acknowledging the significance of establishing a nurturing and empowering setting for learners. Leaders who facilitate transformation prioritize the requirements and welfare of students and endeavour to foster an environment characterized by regard, inclusivity, and cooperation within their educational institutions.

Emphasis on Professional Development: To stay abreast of the swiftly evolving realm of education, administrators are assigning a heightened significance to professional advancement and the perpetual acquisition of knowledge for instructors and personnel. Progressive leaders allocate resources toward the enhancement and progression of their team constituents, rendering occasions for instruction, guidance, and cooperation.

Advancements in Technology: The incorporation of technology in the realm of education has resulted in a significant overhaul in the methods by which students acquire knowledge and educators impart instruction. Leaders with a transformative approach are utilizing technology as a means to enrich pedagogical strategies, foster creativity and novel approaches, and enhance the overall educational achievements of every student (Almalki et al., 2017).

Diversity and Inclusion: As the diversity of educational institutions expands, administrators are increasingly acknowledging the significance of establishing comprehensive and fair learning environments. Visionary leaders are devoted to cultivating diversity, equity, and inclusion within their educational institutions, and endeavour to engender an atmosphere of regard, acceptance, and affiliation for all students and staff.

From Reactive to Proactive Leadership: Shifts and Trends in Educational Leadership

Reactive leadership may be delineated as a style of leadership that exhibits a responsive and proactive methodology, in which leaders tend to tackle issues as they emerge instead of proactively prognosticating and obviating them in advance. This specific method frequently leads to the implementation of temporary remedies that do not effectively tackle the underlying concerns, thereby resulting in a pattern of recurring issues within educational establishments. Within a reactive leadership model, leaders may choose to wait until problems escalate or become widespread before taking action. Consequently, this can create a sense of disorder and instability within the organization, as leaders are constantly extinguishing proverbial fires instead of devoting their attention to long-term strategic planning and initiatives for improvement. Additionally, a reactive leadership approach can impede innovation and growth, as leaders tend to prioritize the preservation of the existing state of affairs rather than actively driving substantial and meaningful change. The transition from a reactive to a proactive leadership approach in education represents a fundamental evolution in the way educational leaders approach their roles and responsibilities. This specific method frequently leads to the implementation of temporary remedies that do not effectively tackle the underlying concerns, thereby resulting in a pattern of recurring issues within educational establishments. Within a reactive leadership model, leaders may choose to wait until problems escalate or become widespread before taking action. Consequently, this can create a sense of disorder and instability within the organization, as leaders are constantly extinguishing proverbial fires instead of devoting their attention to long-term strategic planning and initiatives for improvement (Akmal et al., 2022). Additionally, a reactive leadership approach can impede innovation and growth, as leaders tend to prioritize the preservation of the existing state of affairs rather than actively driving substantial and meaningful change. The transition from a reactive to a proactive leadership approach in education represents a fundamental evolution in the way educational leaders approach their roles and responsibilities. Leaders can enhance their ability to predict and tackle obstacles, cultivate an environment that encourages creativity and advancement, and prepare their organizations for sustained achievement in an ever-changing and intricate educational framework by adopting a forward-thinking approach. As educational leaders continue to adapt to changing trends and demands, cultivating proactive leadership skills will be essential for driving positive change and transformation within educational institutions. This shift has been influenced by various trends and changes in the educational landscape, shaping the way leaders envision and enact their roles in driving positive change within educational institutions. Understanding this transformation is crucial for current and aspiring educational leaders as they navigate the complexities of the modern educational environment.

In response to the limitations of reactive leadership, there was a noticeable shift in the direction of proactive leadership within the area of education. Proactive leadership is characterised by an ahead-wondering and anticipatory technique, where leaders actively searching for to discover and cope with capability-demanding situations earlier than they boost. This proactive stance enables leaders to take an extra strategic and preventative approach to problem-solving, main to greater sustainable and powerful answers. Proactive educational leaders prioritize continuous improvement and innovation, searching for expected future trends and challenges to put their establishments for fulfilment. By fostering a subculture of foresight and strategic planning, proactive leaders empower their teams to adapt to growth and proactively deal with emerging problems. This technique now not only complements organizational resilience but also fosters a lifestyle of collaboration, creativity, and continuous growth (Adeba et al., 2023).

Several key trends and shifts within the educational landscape have contributed to the upward thrust of proactive leadership inside educational institutions. One such model is the increasing complexity and volatility of the educational surroundings, driven by using elements including technological advancements, demographic changes, and evolving pedagogical practices. In this hastily changing panorama, proactive leaders are more prepared to navigate uncertainty and lead their institutions toward sustainable fulfilment. Another model shaping proactive leadership is the developing emphasis on statistics-pushed decision-making and proof-based practices in education. Proactive leaders leverage information and research to tell their strategic making plans and decision-making tactics, permitting them to perceive tendencies, anticipate challenges, and degree the effect in their projects. By embracing a tradition of continuously gaining knowledge and improvement, proactive leaders create a foundation for sustainable growth and innovation within their organizations.

Chapter 3: Theoretical Frameworks for Transformative Leadership

Transformative leadership is a leadership style focused on inspiring and empowering followers to achieve higher levels of performance and personal growth. It goes beyond transactional or transactional leadership, which primarily involves exchanges of rewards and punishments, and even beyond transformational leadership, which focuses on motivating followers through vision and charisma. Transformative leadership seeks to create profound and lasting change by challenging the status quo and fostering innovation, collaboration, and personal development among followers.

Several theoretical frameworks have been proposed to understand and implement transformative leadership effectively:

Bass's Transformational Leadership Theory: Bernard Bass introduced this theory, emphasizing the leader's ability to inspire and motivate followers through a compelling vision, intellectual stimulation, individualized consideration, and idealized influence. Transformational leaders inspire trust and loyalty among followers, encouraging them to transcend their self-interests for the collective good.

Full Range Leadership Model: Building on Bass's work, the Full Range Leadership Model categorizes leadership behaviors into three main styles: transformational, transactional, and laissez-faire. Transformational leadership is characterized by idealized influence, inspirational motivation, intellectual stimulation, and individualized consideration. Transactional leadership involves contingent rewards and management-by-exception, while laissez-faire leadership is characterized by a lack of leadership involvement.

Servant Leadership Theory: Servant leadership emphasizes the leader's role as a servant to their followers, prioritizing their needs, development, and well-being. Servant leaders focus on empowering others, fostering a supportive environment, and promoting a culture of collaboration and service (Lebrón & Tabak, 2018).

Authentic Leadership Theory: Authentic leadership theory emphasizes the importance of self-awareness, transparency, and moral integrity in leadership. Authentic leaders are genuine, honest, and aligned with their values, inspiring trust and loyalty among followers through their consistent behavior and ethical decision-making.

Leader-Member Exchange (LMX) Theory: LMX theory focuses on the quality of the relationship between leaders and followers, suggesting that leaders develop unique exchange relationships with each follower based on trust, mutual respect, and reciprocity. In high-quality LMX relationships, followers are more likely to demonstrate commitment, satisfaction, and performance.

Adaptive Leadership Theory: Adaptive leadership theory emphasizes the leader's ability to navigate complex and dynamic environments by facilitating adaptive change. Adaptive leaders mobilize followers to confront challenges, experiment with new approaches, and learn from failures, ultimately driving organizational resilience and innovation.

These theoretical frameworks provide valuable insights into the principles, practices, and outcomes of transformative leadership, offering guidance for leaders seeking to create positive change and foster growth within their organizations and communities.

Transformational Leadership

Transformational leadership is a dynamic and influential approach to leadership that focuses on inspiring and motivating followers to achieve extraordinary outcomes. It involves the leader working with their team to identify needed change, creating a vision to guide the change through inspiration, and executing the change in tandem with committed members of a group (Al-Mansoori & Koç, 2019). Here's a detailed breakdown of transformational leadership:

1. Vision and Inspiration:

Transformational leaders have a clear vision of the future, inspiring and motivating others. They communicate this vision effectively, painting a vivid picture of what success looks like and how it aligns with the team's or organisation's values and aspirations. By appealing to their followers' higher ideals and values, transformational leaders create a sense of purpose and direction that transcends immediate goals.

2. Intellectual Stimulation:

These leaders encourage innovation and creativity within their teams. They challenge assumptions, foster a culture of critical thinking, and promote problem-solving skills. By encouraging their followers to think outside the box and explore new ideas, transformational leaders stimulate intellectual growth and help their teams adapt to changing circumstances.

3. Individualized Consideration:

Transformational leaders pay attention to the individual needs and concerns of their followers. They act as mentors, providing support and encouragement to help each person reach their full potential. By showing genuine care and empathy, these leaders build strong relationships based on trust and mutual respect, which fosters loyalty and commitment among team members.

4. Charisma and Influence:

Transformational leaders often possess charismatic qualities that attract and inspire others. They have a compelling presence and the ability to articulate their vision in a way that captivates their audience. Through their charisma and persuasive communication skills, they are able to rally support for their vision and mobilize their followers to action.

5. Role Modeling:

These leaders lead by example, embodying the values and behaviors they espouse. They demonstrate integrity, authenticity, and a strong work ethic, serving as a role model for their followers. By practicing what they preach, transformational leaders earn the respect and admiration of their team members, who are more likely to emulate their behavior (Gretzel & Bowser, 2013).

6. Empowerment and Delegation:

Transformational leaders empower their followers by delegating authority and decision-making responsibilities. They trust their team members to take ownership of their work and make meaningful contributions to the organization. By giving people the autonomy to innovate and take risks, these leaders foster a sense of ownership and accountability that leads to higher levels of engagement and performance.

7. Continuous Improvement:

Transformational leadership is not static; it is a continuous process of growth and development. These leaders are always seeking opportunities to improve themselves and their teams. They solicit feedback, reflect on their experiences, and actively seek out new knowledge and skills. By embracing a mindset of continuous improvement, transformational leaders inspire others to do the same, creating a culture of learning and innovation within their organizations.

Benefits of Transformational Leadership:

- Increased Motivation and Engagement: Transformational leaders inspire a sense of purpose and passion in their followers, leading to higher levels of motivation and engagement.
- Improved Performance: By setting high expectations and providing support and encouragement, transformational leaders can help their teams achieve higher levels of performance and productivity.
- Enhanced Creativity and Innovation: By fostering a culture of intellectual stimulation and empowerment, transformational leaders encourage creativity and innovation, leading to new ideas and solutions.
- Stronger Relationships: Transformational leaders build strong, trusting relationships with their followers, creating a sense of loyalty and commitment that leads to greater cohesion and collaboration within teams.
- Adaptability and Resilience: Transformational leaders help their teams adapt to change and overcome challenges by promoting a culture of continuous improvement and learning.

In summary, transformational leadership is a powerful approach to leadership that focuses on inspiring and empowering others to achieve extraordinary results. By articulating a compelling vision, fostering innovation and creativity, and building strong relationships based on trust and respect, transformational leaders are able to motivate their followers to reach their full potential and achieve collective success.

Authentic Leadership

Authentic leadership is a contemporary approach that emphasises leaders' genuineness, transparency, and integrity in their interactions with followers. It's about being true to oneself, leading with honesty, and building trust through sincere relationships. Here's a detailed exploration of authentic leadership:

1. Self-Awareness:

Authentic leadership begins with self-awareness. Leaders who practice authenticity are deeply aware of their values, strengths, weaknesses, and emotions. They clearly understand their beliefs and principles, which guides their decision-making and behavior (Bull et al., 2019). By being introspective and self-reflective, authentic leaders develop a strong sense of identity and purpose.

2. Transparency and Honesty:

Authentic leaders are transparent and honest in their communication. They openly share information, admit mistakes, and express their thoughts and feelings genuinely. By being forthright and transparent, these leaders build trust and credibility with their followers, who appreciate their sincerity and integrity.

3. Consistency:

Authentic leaders are consistent in their words and actions. They align their behaviors with their values and principles, demonstrating integrity and reliability in all situations. By being consistent, these leaders earn the trust and respect of their followers, who rely on them to uphold their commitments and promises.

4. Relational Transparency:

Authentic leaders foster open and honest relationships with their followers. They create a safe and supportive environment where people feel comfortable expressing themselves and sharing their ideas and concerns. By being approachable and empathetic, these leaders build strong connections with their teams, which fosters collaboration and teamwork.

5. Ethical Leadership:

Authentic leaders adhere to high ethical standards in their decision-making and behavior. They prioritize doing what is right over what is expedient, even when faced with difficult choices. By demonstrating ethical leadership, these leaders set a positive example for their followers and create a culture of integrity and trust within their organizations.

6. Emotional Intelligence:

Authentic leaders possess high levels of emotional intelligence. They are attuned to their own emotions and the emotions of others, which allows them to navigate complex interpersonal dynamics with empathy and understanding. By showing empathy and compassion, these leaders create a supportive and inclusive work environment where people feel valued and respected.

7. Purpose and Meaning:

Authentic leaders are driven by a sense of purpose and meaning beyond personal gain. They are passionate about their work and committed to making a positive impact on others and society as a whole. By inspiring others with their vision and purpose, these leaders motivate their followers to strive for excellence and contribute to a greater cause.

Benefits of Authentic Leadership:

- Trust and Credibility: Authentic leaders build trust and credibility with their followers through honesty, transparency, and consistency.
- Employee Engagement: By fostering open and honest relationships, authentic leaders create a supportive work environment where employees feel valued and engaged.
- Ethical Decision-Making: Authentic leaders prioritize ethical considerations in their decision-making, which helps to ensure integrity and fairness within their organizations.
- Organizational Culture: Authentic leaders shape the culture of their organizations by setting a positive example and promoting values such as honesty, transparency, and integrity.
- Personal Growth: Authentic leadership encourages self-awareness and personal growth, as leaders continuously reflect on their values, beliefs, and behaviors.

In summary, authentic leadership is a values-based approach to leadership that emphasizes honesty, transparency, integrity, and relational transparency. By being true to themselves, building genuine relationships, and leading with integrity, authentic leaders inspire trust and credibility, foster employee engagement, and create a positive organizational culture conducive to success and growth.

Distributed Leadership

Distributed leadership is a contemporary leadership model that emphasizes the decentralization of leadership responsibilities across various levels and individuals within an organization. Instead of relying solely on one designated leader, distributed leadership recognizes that leadership can emerge from multiple sources and that effective leadership can be distributed among individuals or teams throughout the organization. Here's a detailed exploration of distributed leadership:

1. Shared Leadership Responsibilities:

In distributed leadership, leadership responsibilities are shared among individuals or teams throughout the organization, rather than being centralized in one person or a small group of leaders. This approach recognizes that leadership skills and expertise exist at all levels of the organization and that different individuals may possess unique strengths and capabilities that contribute to the overall leadership function.

2. Collaborative Decision-Making:

Distributed leadership encourages collaborative decision-making processes where input is sought from various stakeholders across the organization. By involving individuals from different departments, levels, and backgrounds in decision-making, organizations can benefit from diverse perspectives and expertise, leading to more informed and effective decisions.

3. Empowerment and Autonomy:

Distributed leadership empowers individuals and teams to take initiative and make decisions within their areas of expertise. By providing autonomy and encouraging innovation, organizations tap into the full potential of their employees and foster a culture of ownership and accountability. This empowerment helps to unleash creativity and initiative throughout the organization, leading to increased engagement and performance.

4. Adaptability and Resilience:

Distributed leadership enhances organizational adaptability and resilience by decentralizing decision-making authority. Instead of relying on a single leader to navigate complex challenges and opportunities, distributed leadership allows for more agile responses to changing circumstances. Teams and individuals are better equipped to respond quickly to emerging issues and capitalize on new opportunities, leading to increased organizational agility and competitiveness.

5. Developing Leadership Capacity:

Distributed leadership promotes the development of leadership capacity at all levels of the organization. By providing opportunities for individuals to take on leadership roles and responsibilities, organizations cultivate a pipeline of future leaders and ensure continuity in leadership succession. This approach to leadership development helps to build a culture of leadership excellence and promotes long-term organizational sustainability.

6. Enhanced Employee Engagement:

Distributed leadership fosters a sense of ownership and empowerment among employees, leading to increased engagement and satisfaction. When individuals are given the opportunity to contribute to decision-making and take on leadership roles, they feel valued and respected, which strengthens their commitment to the organization. This increased engagement can lead to higher levels of productivity, creativity, and employee retention.

7. Alignment with Organizational Values:

Distributed leadership is aligned with the values of inclusivity, collaboration, and transparency. By involving employees in decision-making and empowering them to lead, organizations demonstrate a commitment to fairness, equity, and respect. This alignment with organizational values helps to build trust and cohesion among employees, leading to a more positive and supportive work environment.

Benefits of Distributed Leadership:

Enhanced Decision-Making: By tapping into the collective wisdom and expertise of multiple individuals, distributed leadership leads to more informed and effective decision-making.

Increased Agility: Decentralizing leadership responsibilities allows organizations to respond more quickly and flexibly to changing circumstances and market dynamics.

Improved Employee Engagement: Empowering employees to take on leadership roles increases their sense of ownership and commitment to the organization, leading to higher levels of engagement and satisfaction.

Leadership Development: Distributed leadership promotes the development of leadership skills and capacities at all levels of the organization, ensuring a strong pipeline of future leaders.

Organizational Resilience: By distributing leadership responsibilities, organizations become more resilient and adaptable to challenges, leading to greater long-term sustainability and success.

In summary, distributed leadership is a flexible and inclusive leadership model that recognizes the collective leadership potential of individuals and teams throughout the organization. By sharing leadership responsibilities, empowering employees, and fostering a culture of collaboration and innovation, organizations can leverage the full potential of their workforce and achieve sustainable success in today's dynamic and complex business environment.

Chapter 4: Case Studies in Transformative Leadership

Case Study 1: Jaime Escalante - Transformative Leadership in Education

Background:

Jaime Escalante was a Bolivian-American educator known for his transformative leadership at Garfield High School in East Los Angeles, California, during the 1980s. He is renowned for his work in teaching advanced mathematics to disadvantaged students and inspiring them to excel academically.

Key Elements of Transformative Leadership:

Vision and Inspiration: Escalante had a vision of academic excellence for his students, despite the challenges they faced. He believed that with hard work, dedication, and high expectations, his students could achieve great success in mathematics and beyond.

Empowerment and Delegation: Escalante empowered his students by believing in their potential and challenging them to push beyond their perceived limits. He delegated responsibilities to them, allowing them to take ownership of their learning and academic success.

Intellectual Stimulation: Escalante fostered a culture of intellectual stimulation in his classroom, encouraging students to think critically, ask questions, and explore mathematical concepts in depth. He challenged them to tackle advanced coursework and exams, such as the Advanced Placement (AP) Calculus exam, which was uncommon in inner-city schools at the time.

Role Modeling: Escalante led by example, demonstrating a strong work ethic, passion for teaching, and unwavering commitment to his students' success. He showed them that with perseverance and determination, they could overcome obstacles and achieve their goals.

Community Engagement: Escalante actively engaged with the local community, parents, and school administrators to garner support for his students and the school's academic programs. He organized tutoring sessions, study groups, and parent-teacher conferences to ensure that students had the resources and support they needed to succeed.

Impact:

Under Escalante's transformative leadership, Garfield High School became known for its exceptional mathematics program and academic achievements. His students, many of whom were from low-income, minority backgrounds, defied expectations and excelled on the AP Calculus exam, with some even earning top scores. Escalante's work inspired a generation of educators and students, demonstrating the transformative power of high expectations, dedication, and belief in students' potential.

Case Study 2: Michelle Rhee - Transformative Leadership in Education

Background:

Michelle Rhee served as the Chancellor of the District of Columbia Public Schools (DCPS) from 2007 to 2010. She implemented ambitious reforms aimed at improving student achievement and transforming the district's struggling education system.

Key Elements of Transformative Leadership:

Visionary Leadership: Rhee had a vision of excellence for DCPS, driven by a belief that all students, regardless of background or zip code, deserved access to a high-quality education. She set ambitious goals for student achievement and held herself and others accountable for results.

Data-Driven Decision-Making: Rhee used data to inform her decision-making and measure progress towards academic goals. She implemented standardized testing and performance metrics to track student achievement, teacher effectiveness, and school performance, allowing for targeted interventions and support.

Bold Reforms: Rhee implemented bold reforms aimed at improving teacher quality, increasing accountability, and driving innovation in teaching and learning. She introduced performance-based pay for teachers, closed underperforming schools, and expanded school choice options, including the opening of charter schools.

Courageous Leadership: Rhee faced significant resistance and controversy during her tenure, particularly from teachers' unions and community members opposed to her reform agenda. Despite facing criticism and pushback, she remained steadfast in her commitment to improving educational outcomes for students and pursued her vision with determination and resolve.

Community Engagement: Rhee engaged with a wide range of stakeholders, including parents, educators, policymakers, and community leaders, to build support for her reform efforts. She sought input and feedback from stakeholders, communicated transparently about her goals and strategies, and worked collaboratively to implement reforms that would benefit all students.

Impact:

Rhee's transformative leadership had a significant impact on DCPS, leading to improvements in student achievement, teacher effectiveness, and overall school performance. While her tenure was marked by controversy and debate, her reforms laid the foundation for long-term improvements in the district's education system. Rhee's work sparked national conversations about education reform and inspired other leaders to pursue bold, innovative approaches to improving student outcomes.

These case studies highlight the transformative power of visionary leadership, bold reforms, and community engagement in driving positive change in education. Leaders like Jaime Escalante and Michelle Rhee demonstrate that with dedication, courage, and a clear vision for excellence, transformative leadership can make a lasting impact on students, schools, and communities.

Case Study 3: Dr. Howard Fuller - Transformative Leadership in Education

Background:

Dr. Howard Fuller is an educator, civil rights activist, and advocate for school choice and educational equity. He is known for his transformative leadership in advocating for educational opportunities for underserved communities, particularly through the charter school movement.

Key Elements of Transformative Leadership:

Advocacy for Equity: Fuller has been a lifelong advocate for educational equity and social justice, particularly for African American and low-income communities. He has worked tirelessly to ensure that all children have access to high-quality education regardless of their background or socioeconomic status.

Founding Charter Schools: Fuller played a key role in the founding of several charter schools, including the Milwaukee Collegiate Academy and the Harambee Community School in Milwaukee, Wisconsin. These schools provide alternative educational options for students in underserved communities and emphasize academic excellence, character development, and community engagement.

Empowerment of Parents and Communities: Fuller believes in empowering parents and communities to take an active role in their children's education. He has been a vocal advocate for school choice policies that give parents the freedom to choose the best educational options for their children, including traditional public schools, charter schools, and private schools.

Collaborative Partnerships: Fuller has worked collaboratively with educators, policymakers, community leaders, and philanthropic organizations to advance his vision of educational equity and excellence. He has formed partnerships with a diverse range of stakeholders to develop innovative solutions to the challenges facing underserved communities.

Leadership in Education Reform: Fuller has been a leading voice in the education reform movement, advocating for policies and practices that prioritize the needs of students and families. He has served on numerous boards and commissions related to education policy and has been a sought-after speaker and advisor on issues of educational equity and social justice.

Impact:

Dr. Howard Fuller's transformative leadership has had a profound impact on the education landscape, particularly in underserved communities. His advocacy for school choice and charter schools has provided educational opportunities for thousands of students who might otherwise have been left behind by the traditional public school system. By empowering parents, advocating for equity, and promoting collaborative partnerships, Fuller has helped to create a more inclusive and equitable education system that better serves the needs of all students.

Case Study 4: Geoffrey Canada - Transformative Leadership in Education

Background:

Geoffrey Canada is an educator, social activist, and founder of the Harlem Children's Zone (HCZ), a comprehensive community organization aimed at improving the lives of children and families in Harlem, New York City.

Key Elements of Transformative Leadership:

Comprehensive Community Approach: Canada's transformative leadership is characterized by his comprehensive approach to addressing the complex challenges facing children and families in underserved communities. The HCZ provides a wide range of programs and services, including early childhood education, after-school programs, family support services, and community development initiatives.

Focus on Education: Education is at the heart of Canada's work with the HCZ. He believes that providing children with a high-quality education is the key to breaking the cycle of poverty and empowering them to reach their full potential. The HCZ's charter schools, Promise Academy I and II, offer a rigorous academic curriculum, extended learning opportunities, and wraparound support services to help students succeed.

Data-Driven Decision-Making: Canada uses data to inform his decision-making and measure the impact of the HCZ's programs and services. By collecting and analyzing data on student outcomes, family needs, and community demographics, he is able to identify areas of strength and areas for improvement, leading to more effective and targeted interventions.

Collaborative Partnerships: Canada has forged partnerships with a wide range of stakeholders, including government agencies, nonprofit organizations, philanthropic foundations, and local businesses. These partnerships help to leverage resources, expertise, and support for the HCZ's programs and initiatives, leading to greater impact and sustainability.

Leadership in the Education Reform Movement: Canada is a recognized leader in the education reform movement, advocating for policies and practices that prioritize the needs of children and families in underserved communities. He has been a vocal proponent of community-based approaches to education reform and has worked to inspire and mobilize others to join the fight for educational equity and social justice.

Impact:

Geoffrey Canada's transformative leadership has had a transformative impact on the lives of children and families in Harlem and beyond. Through his visionary leadership, the Harlem Children's Zone has become a national model for comprehensive community development and education reform. By providing children with access to high-quality education, comprehensive support services, and a nurturing community environment, Canada has helped to break the cycle of poverty and create pathways to success for generations of children. His work has inspired educators, policymakers, and advocates across the country to pursue similar approaches to addressing the root causes of educational inequity and building a more just and equitable society.

Challenges and Lessons Learned

Let's explore some common challenges faced by transformative leaders in education, along with the lessons learned from addressing these challenges:

Challenges:

Resistance to Change: Implementing transformative reforms in education often faces resistance from various stakeholders, including teachers' unions, administrators, and community members who may be hesitant to embrace new approaches or policies.

Resource Constraints: Limited funding and resources can pose significant challenges to transformative leaders, especially when trying to implement ambitious reforms or provide comprehensive support services to students and families.

Equity and Access: Addressing educational inequities and ensuring access to high-quality education for all students, particularly those from underserved communities, can be a complex and ongoing challenge.

Policy and Political Dynamics: Transformative leaders in education must navigate a complex landscape of education policies, regulations, and political dynamics that can impact their ability to implement reforms and drive positive change.

Data Management and Analysis: Effective data management and analysis are essential for informing decision-making and measuring the impact of transformative initiatives. However, collecting, analyzing, and interpreting data can be challenging, particularly in resource-constrained environments.

Community Engagement: Building trust and buy-in from parents, community members, and other stakeholders is crucial for the success of transformative initiatives. However, engaging diverse communities and addressing their needs and concerns requires time, effort, and effective communication strategies.

Sustainability and Scale: Ensuring the long-term sustainability and scalability of transformative reforms can be challenging, especially when relying on external funding or navigating changes in leadership and political priorities.

Lessons Learned:

Build Coalitions and Partnerships: Transformative leaders in education should build coalitions and partnerships with diverse stakeholders, including educators, policymakers, community leaders, and philanthropic organizations, to garner support for their initiatives and leverage resources and expertise.

Communicate Vision and Benefits: Effective communication is key to overcoming resistance to change and building buy-in from stakeholders. Transformative leaders should clearly communicate their vision, goals, and the potential benefits of their initiatives to inspire and motivate others to join the effort.

Focus on Equity and Inclusion: Addressing educational inequities and ensuring access to high-quality education for all students should be a central focus of transformative leadership. Leaders should prioritize equity and inclusion in their policies, practices, and decision-making processes.

Embrace Data-Informed Decision-Making: Transformative leaders should embrace data-informed decision-making to track progress, identify areas for improvement, and measure the impact of their initiatives. Investing in data collection, analysis, and reporting systems can help leaders make informed decisions and drive continuous improvement.

Empower and Invest in Educators: Transformative leaders should empower and invest in educators by providing professional development opportunities, resources, and support to enhance their skills and effectiveness. Building a culture of collaboration, trust, and continuous learning among educators is essential for driving positive change.

Engage with Communities: Transformative leaders should actively engage with parents, community members, and other stakeholders to understand their needs and concerns, build trust and partnerships, and co-create solutions that address local challenges and opportunities.

Plan for Sustainability: Transformative leaders should plan for the long-term sustainability and scalability of their initiatives by seeking sustainable funding sources, building capacity within organizations and communities, and fostering a culture of innovation and adaptability.

Conclusion:

Transformative leadership in education involves addressing complex challenges and driving positive change to improve outcomes for students, educators, and communities. By embracing lessons learned from past experiences and adopting strategies to overcome common challenges, transformative leaders can create lasting impact and drive meaningful progress towards educational equity and excellence.

Chapter 5: The Impact of Transformative Leadership on School Culture

Varied theories on transformational leadership in education draw attention to the efficiency of a couple of years and having the ability to give drive to extra better alternatives and form school life. Further reflection into the impact of the transformational leader on the life of the school is that there is more insight into the prime position where leaders avail themselves of supportive, inclusive, and dynamic surroundings within educational institutions. The very gist of transformative leadership stands on the basis that leaders have the power and ability to inspire and empower people to their best potential expression. In line with this, traditional leadership majors in the maintenance of the status quo while transformative leadership remains future-oriented and capable of initiating the necessary change. A visionary: A Transformational leader develops a common collective vision of the school in the future and affects change by helping to inspire others to work closer so that the goals for the school and visions become a reality. Transformative leadership fundamentally defines school culture that is practised through networking, collaboration, and continuous improvement. Leaders using a transformative approach make available an environment where every stakeholder perceives himself or herself as being regarded and supported in contributing toward the success of the school.

One of the principal manners within which transformative leadership affects the shape of college tradition is in the assistance provided toward the lifestyle of agreement and transparency. Under transforming leadership, values such as open communication, honesty, and integrity would be upheld to help further foster this consideration among groups of workers, students, and parents. This consideration sub-culture will form a base for teamwork, innovation, and respect in the whole schooling community. The other major basics related to transformative leadership include empowerment of others. They understand individual differences and unique requisites and at all times work out the best opportunities for professional development and improvement. By nature, a way of empowering life boosts higher self-confidence, creativity, and motivation towards more consistent productivity among all members of the team through attaining goals. The other thing is that transformative leadership has a big significance on the diversity and inclusivity of the schools' culture, upon which to uphold this to all in the institution. Transformative leadership opens up friendly and welcoming environments that give value and belief to all. The subculture of an appreciation, empathy, and knowledge-taking approach by transformative leadership celebrates diversity in which particular views are given space to be embraced. The role of transformative leadership is quite vast in eradicating the growth culture that characterizes academic institutions. This would mean that the transformative leader sets strong expectations for staff, espouses innovation, and readily accepts a growth attitude in anyone who may work with and around the leader. Along the same line, those schools that are very adaptable to the changing needs and challenges take on a vision of openness toward continuous development to remain effective and relevant in the changing educational setting.

1.   Building a Positive and Inclusive School Environment

Another characteristic that stands out with transformative leadership is its emphasis on building and generating a positive and integrated learning environment. It presents the creation of an open, caring structure where all the people within are valued, appreciated, and helped in the growing process. If they find a background of safety, care, and protection in their school, students will certainly be less averse to academic activities and learning experiences. A high standards and inclusive school culture will have a spread effect on the sense of belonging, motivating scholars to improve their academic standing, take risks in studies, ask questions, and independently engage in classroom discussion. Thereby, educational performance is improved as students have an urge to keep their standard and realize their full potential. High-quality and inclusive school environments support the development of students' social and emotional well-being directly, in line with developing a meaningful sense of community, empathy towards others, and understanding between peers. It ensures that when the student's actual needs are recognized and valued for who they are, he will be polite, friendly, and easy to talk to in any situation leading to the interaction of people, or they will be in a position to form better people skills and relation establishment. This will further contribute to creating a supportive and caring school network in which students will feel that they have the emotional stability to control pressure and adversity successfully.

The inclusive school makes its students an environment that is part and parcel to its being an anti-bullying and misbehaviour initiative institution. It is when inclusions, equity, and mutual recognition are valued in schools that it presents a subculture that values diversity and promotes care and compassion. Students thereby are likely not to indulge less in acts of bullying or discriminatory behaviour once they get the feeling of being part of their fellow beings and are made to appraise the value of how others should feel in respect and kindness. Schools that engage in effective relationships and a climate of recognition can right the reductionist period of bullying, thus presenting a safe and congenial learning climate for all learners. It is a tidy and holistic educational climate that helps to engender benefits not only for the students but also for the locality and relationships with links to the parents and wider community. This approach makes sure that when educational institutions start concentrating on programs that are inclusive and a lot more collaborative, the parents feel that their offspring's educational process is their property and devotion. Parents are not very interested in supporting the education and development of their children by participating in school events, different faculties, and liaising with the teachers and principals. Moreover, community members will not engage but rather will be hit hard and feel the sting of the discarding and difficult-to-reach culture of the school. With the increased engagement, a feeling of cohabitation between the school and the parents and community is inculcated into the learning environment.

1.2. Strategies for Building a Positive and Inclusive School Environment

Educational leadership can bring about the promotion of community, togetherness, and, most of all, dignity in the school environment through alternative thinking and new methods. It is diversity and inclusion that is the basic guideline leading the way to a quality, accommodating school environment. Saluting the very differences in the backgrounds, cultures, and opinions of the students and staff can make educational steering possible. They should be in a position to catalyze all kinds of activities, seminars, and games that depict the school members' diversity and inclusion. Through social inclusion, leaders can find a platform on which to create secure and safe realms in which everyone enjoys being valued and honoured in every aspect. Good communication is of utmost significance in creating a good school sub-culture. Among many other calls to action, good open and honest communication is another that educational leaders should champion among students, teachers, parents, and all interest parties. Through active listening, feedback, and encouraging speaking for itself by the School Network, the leaders can build a culture of consideration and collaboration. In developing sound relationships and partnerships, the leaders will be in a position to encourage teamwork, cooperation, and respect in all contributors to the School Network. Other key ways of building a great and encompassing school environment include building teamwork and empowering educators. This observable engagement will be created by educational leaders supporting professional development through tools and resources that can aid in development and establish a ground for bringing to life the culture of learning and future improvement. This way, it will create an enabling ground, empowering the educators and groups to assert and claim ownership of the work and create a good feeling of team spirit, independence, and empowerment. At the end of the day, this will breed job satisfaction, motivation, and productivity for the students and the school community in general.

Most importantly, promoting the growth of social and emotional learning (SEL) for children to develop into students becomes paramount for propelling an exceptional and all-encompassing educational environment. An SEL package, initiatives, and practices can inroad the schooling process to support the emotional health and development of the learners. With teachings in empathy, awareness of self, and relationship-building, this is what is brought to school. This can lead to a paradigm shift in aptitude in studies, behaviour patterns, and overall attitudes among children in school. Education managers must recognize that opportunities and links should be free from bias and should be available to all students on equal footing. It is, indeed, only from a clear articulation and by redressing systemic barriers, biases, and injustices that the leadership team will build a school environment that is just and inclusive. This might also entail the enforcement of policies, practices, and tasks illustrating equity, diversity, and social justice. With the proper support of marginal businesses, challenging stereotypes, and getting an extra simple and fair academic device that benefits students, leaders manage to create the inclusiveness needed to feel welcome. They foster a sense of belonging, community, reputation, and achievement.

2. Fostering Collaborative Learning Communities

Education collaboration is not a buzzword, but an actual principle of how transformative leadership finds its expression in college culture. Thus, educators can set up a collaborative learning community with the aim of keeping open and respectably protecting the learning environment and nurturing each human, highlighting the corresponding human worthiness and value. As we continue to handle these complex environments of modern-day education, collaboration becomes at the forefront to help avail alternatives that will have better chances of working and ensure that we all are spearheaded towards learning what is essential for better perspectives of a better future for all stakeholders in the education environment. Today's dynamics of the fast-changing and evolving education context promote the massive shift from the conventional top-down approach towards inclusive and collaborative forms of leadership. This push is further facilitated by the fact that no single individual is capable of mastering all the knowledge, skills, and abilities necessary to come to terms with the manifold complexities modern educational systems present.

Collaboration in education is important since it can breed a sense of community among and to the participants. When teachers, principals, students, parents, and community residents come together on common grounds and achieve a common goal, they breed a further sense of purpose and unity which further goes beyond their stated interest in whatever subject. This, when shared with everybody, enriches relationships and brings forth a positive and friendly school climate where people feel valued, respected, and listened to. The very act of working together brings forth the ideas and skills that will flow out into developing enhanced ways of problem-solving and decision-making. Practically, the breadth of views of people and the experience combined means that collaborative learning communities can invent new solutions to complex problems in an inventive way adapt more effectively to change and build the capacity in which they practice. The collective knowledge gathered is not for individual schools' benefits, but one that helps exude an impetus and general development in the sector of education. Collaboration is another aspect that influences an increase in a boom and development among credible experts in education. Collaboration is enhanced in the relationship that teachers have through the efficacy of carrying out their work. They proportion what they do, accept critique and are active in learning opportunities. Such will yield the reflection and inquiry-based practice of teachers. Many educators. Where there is collaboratively effective play in coming up with interdisciplinary projects, educators are in a position to address the needs of many learners and have the capability, to implement individualized learning approaches, and being able to develop inclusive classroom ecosystems hence addressing the need for many learners and capabilities. Educatively and collaboratively, educators can offer a comprehensive and highly motivating learning environment which in turn helps learners who take a keen interest in becoming effective problem solvers and critical thinkers, and in their realization, develop into lifelong learners.

2.2. Importance of Collaboration in Education

Collaboration is important for several reasons. Primarily, it necessitates that there is a common basis for all educators, students, and parents toward an improved feeling of support and study. When all parties are involved variably forward to the process of instruction, they are so much better placed to feel attached to the prosperity of the school and its charge. Collaboration also supports professional growth and a culture of constant improvement. Educators can share ideas, pool best practices, and learn from each other because they are each working together toward common purposes. This type of professional learning is highly interactive and thus holds great promise for gaining heightened teacher efficacy, student success, and the fostering of a healthy school life. Such collaboration is equally core to the work in diversity and inclusion in the educational centre. In this way, learning communities through collaboration hold the very promise of an education environment that is just and culturally sensitive through the integration of people with diverse backgrounds, perspectives, and accounts. The collection of people from diverse backgrounds, perspectives, and accounts is promising to assist in creating a more just and culturally sensitive environment of learning. This can be ensured through cooperation in education that bridges the gap between theory and practice. Such collaboration would involve interaction among educators and researchers creating an opportunity for the schools to have more assurance that the practices in which they engage are based on findings about the most current trends in the manner in which schools conduct their business and the most recent changes in the professions relative to their scholarship as practitioners. This type of collaboration between educators and researchers in the issues of curriculum design and implementation would bear teaching strategies that would result in quicker student engagement and far better impacts for all learners.

2.3. Transformative Leadership Strategies for Fostering Collaboration

A transformative leader within a learning community fosters collaboration through communication of vision, clearly setting the goals, and handing power over to the stakeholder groups to take charge of their learning and development. Some of the strategies applied by the transformative leader in the promotion of collaboration within educational settings include:

1. *Building Trust and Relationships*: Transformative leadership philosophy upholds the building, considering, and nurturing excellent relationships between stakeholders. Leaders create a

supporting and inclusive environment under which a sense of psychological safety arises, easy conversation, risk-taking, and experimenting are elicited. People working jointly toward common goals do so out of trust – this is the basis for fruitful cooperation and not necessarily agreement.

2. ***Encouragement of Shared Leadership and Decision-Making***: Transformative leaders help educators to share leadership tasks, and responsibility of decision-making, and contribute their knowledge in the creation of new school vision, fostering creativity and foresight. Encouraging distributed leadership would then assist a leader in utilizing diverse talents and perceptions that exist in a group in a manner that fosters cultures of collaboration and innovation, building a sense of ownership and responsibility amongst its stakeholders.

3. ***Facilitate Professional Learning Communities***: Transformational leaders foster the construction of professional knowledge for the groups that the educators come into through dialogical reflective practices, share exemplary practices, and be collaborative in generating research-based holistic strategies to embrace teaching and learning outcomes. It can lead to the opportunity for the continuation of the grafting professional development and the collaboration where greater collective knowledge can be built on, the culture of constant betterment, and effective change in school affected.

4. ***Encouraging Innovation and Creativity***: A transformational leader encourages creativity, experimentation, and innovation in a school setup. Brand establishment encourages the culture of accepting risks, learning from failures, and alternative ways to do something; this gears leaders toward encouraging educators to find new ideas, get innovative strategies, and stretch the margins of traditional approaches in teaching. In an innovation subculture, leaders help to nurture a newfound spirit of curiosity and resilience that is developed in their stakeholders amidst the fellow rapidly changing educational landscape.

2.4. Evidence of Successful Collaborative Initiatives

Examples of productive tasks built in cooperation in educational institutions include professional learning communities, teacher collaboration teams, interdisciplinary projects, community partnerships, and so on. A number of the tasks have already proved their effectiveness in raising the level of teacher collaboration, student engagement, and academic success due to the culture of mutual support, inventiveness, and perfection. Some of the insight-oriented researches contribute to a common conclusion that throws light on the beneficial influence of collaborative programs on the students' high achievements, teacher attrition, and school progress. According to Molinillo et al. (2018) study, it was established that communities based on collaboration improved instructional performance, engaged students better, and led to better improvement in social-emotional. Empirical studies such as Hargreaves and Fullan (2012) noted that indeed, there was a direct relation where a collaborative professional learning community linked directly to improved teacher collaboration, consequently leading to job satisfaction and the retention rate. In the subsequent study, Jordan (2020) postulated that collaborative professional learning communities bear a strong relationship in improving job satisfaction, increasing the level of collaboration, and later the rates of teacher retention. Some teachers also mentioned that participation in collaborative activities resulted in more being extended, appreciated, and working with a higher motivation to use new instructional practices and contribute to activities that would support school improvement. Madrid (2016) confirmed that schools with strong cultures of collaboration relentlessly outscore their peers in outputs and indicators of success with students and teacher retention rates. In a nutshell, the schools could portray a way of life based on working together and collective responsibility, proven to denote an empowering and supporting environment for the teachers and students. These findings are further affirmed by other studies which have proved that collaborative learning communities increase teachers' satisfaction in the profession, professional growth, and further enhance job performance through intense involvement in the process of hiring and induction (Knapp et al., 2016; Long et al., 2021). Other researchers with similar reasons supported that teachers who had been involved in collaborative tasks had higher motivation and better levels of efficacy (Li et al., 2022; Canrinus et al., 2012; Klassen & Chiu, 2010). In addition, the joint pursuit of a common goal through teamwork enables the instructors to value and support each other, increasing their morale and work performance. More so, through encouraging the instructors, students, and other stakeholders towards the significant projects and tasks, the college community gets experience of experience of ownership, engagement, and delight. The partnership-based engagements are those that are known to break down silos, bridge cross-disciplinary learning, and with which people are empowered to make a high-impact quality difference in their school and network.

Chapter 6: Innovative Approaches to Professional Development

Chapter 6: Innovative Approaches to Professional Development

In education, continuous professional development ensures that professional development is availed to all teachers to ensure the practice of positively transforming the same for learners to be able to achieve improved results. The more constant cry of a concept such as continuous professional development has had its necessity enhanced for educators to underpin the importance of lifelong learning and growth. It is necessary to equip educators with professional development in that it is capable of equipping the latest methodologies in teaching, the most recent technologies, and the leading-edge changes in education research. They inculcate new behaviour in instruction, develop strategy innovations for the diverse student needs and the educational institution cultivates the spirit of inventiveness. Furthermore, professional development supports improvement in instruction by offering educators an opportunity to think about improved instruction, including their teaching practice and the forms of assessment while providing evidence of strategies to support their students' learning. It equally offers opportunities for these educators to associate with fellow educators, exchange best practices, and carry out meaningful discussions for further professional growth.

Another development in professional development in education is taking place at an increasing rate in the 21st century, where it has become globalized through the interchange of thought and practices by educators all over the world who are busy sharing. This should help with concerns from localism to diversity in the culture, social or economic background in professional development shaping where the educator works. By espousing a global view on professional development, educational managers can borrow innovative practices and strategies as adopted in other parts of the world and shape them to fit into the needed peculiarities of their educational institutions. The more the following trends are outlined, the more they shape the revolution on continuous learning and growth for educators. For example, the emerging trends include the increasing inclination towards personal professional development plans designed according to the needs and objectives that individual educators. It includes technology when it comes to professional development- internet programs, virtual conferencing or meetings, and webinars that make working educators easy and convenient methods of attending classes because such matters can be attended to at flexible hours. This new value that education has assumed has followed social-emotional learning and well-being through the call for an increase in professional development programs that boost educators in helping students build relations with other teachers and learning in an open environment.

1. Traditional Approaches to Professional Development

Professional development is one of the important aspects of quality education and development in teaching practices. Professional Development has for so many years relied on workshops, seminars, conferences, and conventions, but newer innovative approaches are emerging.

1.1 Workshops and Seminars

The workshops and seminars have always remained the favourites to most for their more intensive training in a specific area or field areas. Unlike online training sessions, these traditional training methods are most time organized in a well-centralized environment of learning, and most of these classes are conducted by the most famed professionals. Overall, however, their more intensive structure mutates into greater negatives regarding educator skill enhancement when these workshops and seminars are limited in duration, one-dimensional in their content, and offered without follow-up support. In this regard, new and better innovative approaches to these workshops and seminars are coming out now to work within the generous limitations. Some of those comprise personal professional development plans per educator, leading to all the more meaningful learning. Used besides that are such technologies, interactive online modules, or even simulations in virtual reality.

1.2 Conferences and Conventions

Conferences and conventions group educators of similar focus to exchange ideas, findings, and best practices. It can always avail plenty of ample networking opportunities and the power of learning from different accounts. The only drawback is that conventional conferences and conventions are relatively passive. The following are the innovative means: For example, the program will be designed more participatory in the ways that panel discussions, presentations, and engaging activities can be included in the form of workshops. Similarly, the use of technology such as virtual conferencing platforms or the application of mobile tools results in place networking and carries activities ahead of the physical area of conventional conferences.

1.3 Online Learning Platforms

In this regard, the innovation that the advent and subsequent growth of professional development on electronic and online platforms all gave educators opportunities all over to improve in their respective duties. In most online forums and groups, educators often engage in several avenues for professional development, including online courses and others such as webinars, which all ensure that educators can easily engage in dynamic professional development in a rather accessible manner. Online platforms allow educators to learn, unlearn and relearn at their own pace and trajectory, shaping a personal learning journey that is uniquely suited to their needs and interests. To add to that, most online learning environments will bomb participants with an abundance of messages from various educators that are supplied through their numerous interactive forms, including discussion boards, quiz sections, or even evaluations of each other's efforts. Then, there seems to be a great fusion between educators who value collaboration and sharing. Some of those educators even have badges or certifications on their profiles.

1.4 Peer Coaching and Mentoring

One of the great ways to do professional development is via peer coaching and mentoring so that educators can learn from experiences and wisdom. The latter is more of a process of relationship collaboration involving reciprocity with educators, thereby conciliating a culture of ongoing learning and development. It is this last category that is of particular importance because most of them would be highly structured in nature and possess features of dynamic and innovative peer coaching and mentoring programs, like large ensemble lesson planning, peer observations, or even feedback sessions. The coaching may be either online or conducted in person, based on the convenience and availability of the faculty. Peer coaching and mentoring can pave the way for educators to propose skill development and workplace happiness if just the settings supporting and empowering are laid down for them.

Challenges in Traditional Approaches

The attempts to improve staff professional development, through traditional methodologies, reveal more constraints and challenges the more educational management sets in to implement measures. Among the challenges proving impossible for educators is the issue of insufficiency in time and other resources. In a speedy education environment, finding the time to be involved in the traditional development levels may remain significantly close to impossibility. Secondly, most traditional workshops and seminars impose on the time and financial resources of educators who can ill afford the time away from their day-to-day instruction. Third, personalized learning is not considered in the course of traditional professional development. Educators are diverse and enter the profession with different sets of experience and expertise. The approach to professional development fails to respond to the differences and won't fit so many different educators, this approach varies to the learning needs of assurance of a diverse workforce through a learning context that is contextual and responsive.

The challenge to such issues has now been responded to by educators, by moving towards personalized professional development in education. The targeted path of professional development has helped in the facilitation of targeted learning experiences, which help educators participate in types of content and activities relevant to the individual goals set and aspirations. The ability to include self-paced online courses, virtual coaching, working collaboratively on projects, and more allows a dynamic and engaging environment an educational manager can provide for professional development. One of the oddest things that are among the advantages of personalized professional development is the fact that content can be selected based on the interested party or general growth areas for an educator. In this regard, well-designed opportunities are useful if they personalize and therefore motivate and engage the educated in being able to select from learning opportunities which are most pertinent to them and their needs for professional growth. The idea of educators growing at their speed and being committed to fully internalizing and externalizing this new knowledge and these new skills lies at the heart of personalized learning experiences.

Technology is the key player in enabling personalized professional development activity in an education setup. It provides online forums and tools, gives flexible attendance of educators to professional learning opportunities, and takes away both time and location constraints. Virtual communities and social networking sites were teachers with various peers with whom they share, apply knowledge, and live in a learning-building culture. Moreover, data analytics and artificial intelligence tools will make professional development customized according to the preferences, performance, and feedback of the teachers on their own. Educational managers will for the first time be in a position of monitoring and assessing their staff's learning needs and customizing professional development in a way that will ensure maximum impact and relevance. Other tools include active simulations and even virtual reality experiences, a very emerged learning environment that can be explicitly customized for individual styles of learning and preferences. Although the shift towards entirely tailored professional growth in education is linked with numerous blessings, it also bears a challenging paradox. The educational leader will need to be in a viable position to address the issue of scalability, sustainability, and equity thereof. This can only be felt given a running philosophy of partnership as this exists between the teachers, those in the administration and policy implementers while in the development and implementation of personalized professional growth.

2. Technology-Enhanced Approaches to Professional Development

With the system changing, technology has become an indispensable part for educators and educational managers to remain updated with new aids to teaching technology and methods. Technology has brought technology-enhanced methods of learning for educational manager's experience and innovative learning. They envelop milieus that provide environments of learning and platforms that use digital resources to enhance learning and develop skills. They avail educational management opportunities for professional development that give to their pace and convenient time as opposed to scheduled time geared for face-to-face workshops, and seminars. The technology availed to education managers through the internet varies from giving them access to great resources, sharing their thoughts with other education managers who may be their peers or colleagues even far across the globe, and experiencing interactive training that has been personalized for their very special needs and interests. In a professional development problem for technology-enhanced approaches to professional development, a salient point has to be the customizable learning experiences. Custom areas are understood to deliver training through the most effective approach to learning. There will be online classes, webinars, and virtual conferences from which an education manager can pick out something that suits his professional needs and interests. Personalized participation in educational management has been mainly advantageous to educational managers since they will be able to focus on the areas that they need for skills or knowledge development.

Furthermore, technology-enhanced strategies for professional development bring in an easily accessible avenue of continuous learning for educational managers. In this regard, with access to the internet and round the clock, for online education, or virtual learning, educational managers can develop and update their skills and knowledge to current trends in education. The professional development process is useful equally in that it exposes technological innovations to be beneficial to individual managers, in that it enables the latter to continually improve the ways of learning within their field; among other benefits, it brings improvements in educational practice and results strewn across countries. Another advantage of the technology-enhanced professional development approach is the emphasis that is put on collaboration and networking. By use of technology, social media groups, virtual communities, and other forms make it easy for education managers to be linked to their peers easily to share best practices and even engage in some discussions that will impact professional growth and development. Through technology, such collaborations would be easy and timely in making education managers seize every opportunity to get a wide array of perspectives and insights that make education lively and more effective in being leaders.

Online Courses and Webinars

Several online courses and webinars are evoking a great deal of interest among teachers from different parts of the globe. There is a myriad of benefits associated with likewise technology-aided learning mediums. The benefit of technology-aided learning mediums is the matters of flexibility that the mediums emanate in executing professional development activities. Leaders can execute professional development activities at their pace and convenience programs to be turned discriminately into a strong time-based barrier that characterizes many traditional face-to-face training programs. Moreover, technology offers interactive features like quizzes, discussion boards, and multimedia resources. Educators are endowed with the ability and consequentially in the process of making the process of teaching and learning more interesting.

Virtual Communities of Practice

Virtual communities of practice will have a great role to play in attaining enhanced encouragement, sharing ideas, and professional development pursuits for educators. Online communities are there to join like-minded who share an interest in a subject, toward collaborating and communicating. Virtually driven practice communities enable educators to easily keep in touch, enter into constructive discussion, share resources, solicit suggestions, and reflect on their art of teaching. The interactions also must offer continual professional development to the participants. Virtual communities also help in ensuring that one is well-informed about the latest trends or any new or innovative agenda in education. Thereafter, educators could be able to attend more online discussions and virtual events.

Benefits of Technology-Enhanced Approaches

Technology-enhanced professional development offers enormous and broad benefits from flexibility and accessibility to tailored learning when embraced, technology of improvement in the process of education. Technology affords educators distinction in composition for learning with flexibility and access to professional development activities. With educational leaders modelling the use of innovation, a culture of learning and growth in institutions can only be beneficial in the long run, not only to the educator but to the student. Flexibility and access form the key attributes of technology-enhanced approaches to professional development. Since technology-enhanced approaches do not put limitations on educators at that very level of engagement, they can take part in learning activities at their speed and convenience. Online courses, webinars, and virtual conferences offer professional development easily, irrespective of time and geography. Thus, the flexibility given to the individuals in the case of technology-supported approaches allows them to shape their learning experience according to their requirements and likings. Professional development through technology may be anything from a self-directed online course to an actual real-time virtual conversation. Technology allows for all sorts of media to help a person with professional development, and it can even be self-started into a more informal kind of mentorship.

Such technologically facilitated approaches also offer the needed flexibility and easy access for educators in terms of their missions. The basic professional principle of quality professional development is the assertion that the development activity is first and foremost personally engaging for the educators. Technology plays a huge part in assuring this personal dimension of all development activities through a variety of tools and resources that educators find engaging. In other words, an educator will get the necessary content, which will be of interest and will give good learning outcomes. For example, with technology, it then becomes proportionally much easier for an educator to introduce alluring, interactive, and engaging learning experiences to the classroom through virtual reality simulations or other gamified activities in an attempt to suit various learning styles or even preferences. In so doing, the educational managers bring about the use of technology in personalizing some professional development experiences to the educators who strive to exist and succeed in the change of the quickly-changing educational landscape that our world today offers.

3.   **Collaborative Approaches to Professional Development**

Collaboration was one of the active guiding principles for the educational manager. Professional development will reveal that through collaboration, managers in education will be better placed to share their ideas about issues, best practices, and innovative efforts toward some mutual problem. It is against this background that these collaborative models of professional development for educational managers create a sense of belonging and community among the educational managers themselves or a support network that goes beyond institutional and national boundaries. This sense of belonging assumes greater importance within the context of global education where similar problems and opportunities are shared by educational managers irrespective of where they are located. Professional development to an innovative professional contributes to educational management, cooperating based on a global perspective. In agreement, such a wealth of experience and collective wisdom that educational managers derive from the wide diversity that the world provides could be of assistance in retooling the education sector. They would, through peer observation and feedback from the professional learning communities, give fresh ways toward professional development that provide a new sense to the educational manager looking to make his staff better off in skills and competencies.

The peer observation with feedback strategy has been ranked by many within the practices of professional development as one of the most valued means by which educators practice reflectively and receive constructive input from colleagues. The process involves a teacher observing a peer within the classroom environment, receiving feedback about the observations and the two engage in a discussion that will in turn lead to better and improved practices by the teacher. Thus, the value of peer observation and feedback would serve to enhance the development of a culture on the aspect of how to continuously improve educators. Peer feedback would assist teachers in adopting a new perspective relating to their teaching strategies, identifying areas considered development areas, and experimenting with new strategies in their classes. In addition to that, peer observations create collegiality and collaboration for educators to operate in an environment where professional development is nurtured by collaboration. At the methodology level, this also means that the educational managers bear the higher burden of support and making peer observation and feedback possible to suppose that observance is embedded in the professional development structure. It is upon them that they would take the initiative to set protocols and level recognition in successful revelation emerging from observant processes. Thus, by embedding observations and peer feedback in this professional development infrastructure, they allow educational managers to enhance their capabilities by which their staff will turn into reflective practitioners committed to continuous growth and development.

Indeed, Professional Learning Communities (PLC) have developed as a powerful tradition through which the culture of shared learning and growth has been facilitated in the noble profession education. Thus, it is a collaborative structure for the people in the education sector; equally, opponents constantly listen to each other during the process of improving pedagogy. The advantages of professional learning communities follow: In addition, the educators will get to share their insight and experiences on the issues at hand in as deep a discussion as possible about the issues of teaching and learning. Foundational principles of the PLC will guide educators in acting collaboratively with data towards making decisions and advancing instructional strategies in line with the latest research, and various education trends. Support from the educational manager is in the form of establishing and maintaining professional learning communities, through making adequate provisions for time and other resources necessary in fostering concerted collaboration. A culture of trust, sharing, and respect should also be nurtured within the group that reflects encouraging a spirit of inquiry and innovation towards the issues will greatly help in building the goals of a professional learning community. This will be realized through an investment in the PLCs from the educational managers, who are to provide a dynamic professional development system in an autonomous environment in which the educators are more comfortable and freer to take risks, assisting in learning to work towards the final goal of collective excellence.

Benefits of Collaborative Approaches

The collaborative professional development approach implies that more is added to both teachers' and students' gains from sharing knowledge, ideas, and best practices, and building positive professional relationships. Collaboration means educators, through assuming collaborating approaches and tapping into the collective learning power, get their skills sharpened, acting in the capacity of facilitators of learning to enhance teaching practices, encourage innovations, and in ways contribute to the betterment of educational outcomes.

Professional development would demand that such collaborative approaches be shared at large. This model guarantees that there is a sharing of knowledge and specialization among educators. They have met an opportunity where they can professionally engage, share, promote, and emphasize the best effective teaching principles as well as the best teaching practices or even exchange material relevant to effective teaching and learning engagements. This allows individuals to tap into the collective wisdom of the consortium's diverse group of educators. The consortium also holds that educators who are in traditional schools allow more possibilities for peer learning and mentorship. Such projects and initiatives would ensure the best from each side of the aisle in effecting programmatic collaboration that lays out the best. Such a notion is very knowledge-based and experienced in such collaborations could achieve benefits not just for individual educators but for larger scales in practice in every single instance. Participating in collective activities about professional development gives way to instil, explaining what is new and taking shape in education. Participation in collective activities about professional development empowers educators with expanded knowledge, inculcates new skills within them, and makes them proactive towards the journey of their professional development. It is a continuous process where knowledge and expertise keep adding, it should drive toward innovation and better practices in education all for the betterment of student outcomes.

From the educators' collaboration, joint professional development emphasizes the development of professional networks that jointly become very vital in processing collaboration and mutual supportiveness by educators, therefore creating a feeling of connectedness and solidarity in education. Professional networks can be explained as developed support mechanisms that allow one to seek somebody of the same wavelength as yourself for teaching and direction at both emotional and cognitive testing times. In building firm professional relationships, educators can in turn draw from the collective wisdom and experience of other educators working through otherwise difficult circumstances in developing new ideas and becoming part of the change they wish to see in their educational settings. Moreover, supportive professional networks inspire and motivate teaching faculty to remit the best of their professional role. Since it fosters belonging and camaraderie, it will bring about employee well-being and satisfaction with the job, which will then lead to a positive and conducive work environment.

4.   Culturally Responsive Approaches to Professional Development

What is important in considering culturally responsive professional development is the fact that culture does pattern the way people learn, the way they communicate, and how he or she may relate to others as well. Educational leaders who treasure cultural diversity and correspondingly, draw on culturally salient approaches in and through their work will be far better equipped to plan learning experiences that are more engrossing and effective as regards students in general. Another more recent research study finding shows that culturally responsive professional development can be advantageous to teachers and students alike. Second, appropriate training, evoking cultural contexts and meeting the needs of students culturally, would be in a better position to put educators at the helm to respond, appreciate, and understand their students' varying cultural contexts. Third, the possibility of educational disparities in followers' cultural differences being minimized would be enhanced through culturally responsive professional development. Further, in light of providing educational managers with tools and strategies for the creation of culturally proficient learning environments, the schools will work hard to close the achievement gap and encourage educational equity for most students and all the communities. In plain words, any focus on cultural responsiveness in professional development marks the best progress across the board in the education field. The multicultural nature and culture belonging to the students as much as the educators, if recognized, would make it easy to model a dull learning environment into one that is as captivating and effective for every school community member. In adopting cultural response models, and links with local perspectives, the educational manager allows support for a learning environment that enables educators and learners to strive in a modern world characterized by diversity.

The Significance of Culturally Responsive Approaches

An educational manager is supposed to appreciate and value the various cultural backgrounds of his/her subordinates and students in this era of contemporary living in a multicultural society. Some of the necessities in developing culturally responsive Professional development approaches lie in creating benevolent welcoming settings where all people from any culture or subculture can feel welcomed, appreciated, encouraged, and able to perform and develop at their optimum potential. Educators fit into the student body by helping to create a sense of belonging. This does not only boost morale and engagement but heralds optimal academic outcomes. Generally, culturally responsive professional development efforts tend to assist the educators themselves in gaining attributes or information that will help them effectively support diverse learners and the development of a culturally responsive curriculum. Embracing diversity in professional development would lead to social justice and equity within the corridors of educational institutions. These initiatives that any educational manager shares sum up in bringing down the systematic barriers and working towards a more equal environment for everybody concerned be it something that deals with diversity and inclusion.

Benefits of Culturally Responsive Approaches

The immense gains that come out of adopting culturally responsive approaches are quite beneficial to the professional development of educational managers. The use of culturally responsive professional development approaches is the development of an all-inclusive and equitable educational setting. Infusion of such varied perspectives, pluralities, traditions, and values into pedagogical practice enables educationists to build up a much more inviting and affirming learning environment for students from varied cultural backgrounds, as it does not only give belongingness to the students but also deals with systemic forms of inequalities and biases, that lay within the system. Elevation and making central practices which be responsive to the school culture in professional development programs, particularly an educational manager, should appreciate values which are committed to the changes in the learning landscape that students and staff will experience in totality. Basically, through curriculum development, pedagogical methods, school policy and creation a school educational manager will help contribute towards an air of respect, a positive attitude, and understanding with all participants of the school community.

Another very important contribution that incorporation of the culturally responsive approaches in professional development makes is an improvement in cross-cultural understanding between educators and students. Through the professional development programmes in which educators engage in different cultural perspectives and experiences, they can act in a way that reduces the cultural divides foster and develops empathy, as well as mutual respect among people from distinctly different backgrounds. The cultural coach's co-learner role has assisted the learning managers in the modelling of culturally responsive practice. They supported all educators in accelerating their cultural competence while fostering intercultural dialogue and collaboration.

Chapter 7: Technology and Transformative Leadership

Chapter 7: Technology and Transformative Leadership

Technology has shifted the approach toward the teaching and learning process, offering infinite opportunities in the way educators relate to each other and offer collaboration, creativity, and personalized learning experiences. Probably, the accessibility of educational technology is at an impressively high level at each step, ranging from interactive whiteboards to online learning platforms, all of these to a degree that will hugely impress students and teachers. Engaging various kids' learning styles via digital tools helps to develop more sensitive critical thinking skills and take a closer look at complex ideas. In addition, technology avails a lot of information-based resources much more in quantity, surpassing what one can find in traditional textbooks. In incorporating a transforming leadership model, schools will also prepare and create students given such a dynamic environment for life in the 21st century. With the infusion of technology, education could level the field to democratize knowledge and make active agents out of students in their quest toward learning. All these benefits of technology in education resonate with the call for the execution of technology within an institution. Further outlined in educational technology with transformative leadership extends its adoption of digital tools at the strategic level and also outlines a basic in changing pedagogical practices and organization culture. Inspires innovation fosters a culture of continuous learning and empowers the educator to consider and use knowledge in the environment.

Some of the pivotal duties that a transformative leader in education would need to perform are vision and direction toward technology integration. Their articulation of a clear roadmap on how technology will help in making teaching and learning more effective has stakeholders who support making proper allocations of resources and ensuring sustainability within the technology initiatives. Beyond being change visionaries and agents, transformative leaders must champion change. They inspire, motivate and coax their staff and other stakeholders to embrace best practices and foster a realization culture. In educational technology, the role of the leader is understood more in terms of unwavering support for the development of educators and support in continuing that development. A leader who sponsors and participates in various professional development activities including mentoring opportunities, and collaborative learning communities help prepare and provide knowledge and skills to teachers hence making a powerful use of technology in class. Indeed, investing in staff and emphasizing growth and development to manoeuvre through the complexities of this digital era.

The concepts of transformational leadership and distributed leadership offer so much insight into how the position of leadership is beginning to change regarding the exponential growth of technologies in the educational domain. A range of theoretical models carrying different broad theoretical assumptions could be applied by information or technology leaders to inspire and lead a climate of innovation, collaboration, and empowerment for success in the digital age. A transformational leader in the educational setting is defined to be purposeful, knowing clearly what the problem is and able to articulate a vision for the school. One who inspires and enables others in delivering innovation with a meaning to realize excellence, hence thereby creating a culture of continuously improving. Good relations among teachers, students, parents, and other stakeholders are placed at the core of the process of transformational leadership in education. Through sympathetic behaviour, good listening, and support through proper guidance, transformational leaders give a sense of mutual trust and cooperation in the school. Leaders in the transformational educational paradigm also understand, how to properly utilize technology concerning the improvement in the overall teaching and acquisition process. Instructors will be comfortable in the development of interesting and interactive learning platforms that help learners with personalized learning opportunities. This will support communication enhancing collaboration amongst different stakeholders since digital media enables the development of interoperable content.

In the theory of distributed leadership, the concept is that leadership is distributed over many rather than centred in the hands of one person. Thus, distributed leadership in education involves the sharing of leadership capacities among teachers, students, support staff, and other members in ways that incorporate more decentralized and participative ways of making decisions and addressing matters. Distributed leadership, taken from management and leadership literature once more, makes people feel that they can accomplish leadership at all levels in the organization, amongst other individuals, through ownership and responsibility. Again, the notion of distributed leadership in education recognizes that any organization is always rich in expertise and perspectives, which it would be wise to harness for improvement. This form of leadership, therefore, avails a leader the chance to draw from the collective wisdom of the school community in finding solutions to complex problems, employing great strategies in ensuring the members elicit a culture of learning and improvement.

1.   The Role of Technology in Transformative Leadership

Contrary to earlier thoughts, it was in 2006 when Punya Mishra and Mathew Koehler designed the TPACK (Technological Pedagogical Content Knowledge) framework explaining that effective teaching builds on a deep understanding of how technology and pedagogy interact with each other. The model assumes that effective integration of technology into pedagogical practices should occur at a particular nexus of the three knowledge bases interlocked among the educators, where they purposefully mix their knowledge of technologies with aptitudes in teaching and abilities in subject matter. In this regard, TPACK underpins the model of transformational educational leadership by providing a foundational model for educational leadership to develop new organizational and institutional reforms. It will have inculcated what underpins TPACK, placing the power for transformative leadership such that, in turn, their teachers may operate technological integrations into classroom practices in ways that would see engagement and learning outcomes of the students getting to scale levels like never before.

In this regard, transformative leadership involves encouraging a culture of innovation and collaboration with the teachers. This is brought about through the professional development of the teachers in TPACK knowledge that ultimately makes them able to leverage technology. In other words, this is a process whereby the recognizant leaders are in a position to help teachers venturing into new pedagogical means and easily infuse technology in the curriculum with considerations of a dynamic learning environment that will cater for all the learners. Additional benefits include the ability to make the utilization of technology as a tool of change by these transformative leaders within their institutions. This is because innovative practices can't be inspired if not by leaders who have modeled and who continue to provide consumable support, resources, and time to the staff in a way that encourages the staff to take risks helping them adapt to new technologies and new practices in teaching that can cause transformations to the educational experience of the students.

2.   Challenges of Transformative Leadership in the Digital Age

Technology is providing every opportunity for transformative leadership in education, but on the other end of the continuum, it brings a set of challenges. A major challenge that transformative leaders face is the pace of change with technology because educators are always expected to adapt and continue the upgrading of skills according to emerging trends. This has been compounded in the area of matters of equitable access to technology and other digital resources among the student populace. This also means that transformative leaders shall carry the uphill task of the digital divide and ensure equal opportunities for all students in technology-enabled learning experiences. With the digital age comes a complex set of problems regarding ethics and privacy that would call for careful navigation from transformative leaders. It can be utilized to record data and analyze the performance of students. In all cases, data safety and privacy must be ethically given due consideration. Amidst the many stumbling blocks and hiccups that may be faced along the way, the digital age certainly gives great opportunities for transformational leadership in the education sphere. Technology and innovation bring to life a more vibrant dynamism that lets educators stand in a position to chalk out more interactive and user-friendly methods of learning that shall meet the exact needs of the student. Enable collaboration and creativity between students, availing them with digital tools for the best versions of the learning agenda. In space for virtual work and resources of project management, multimedia resources, easily aid in pooling ideas together, bringing the idea of sharing into fruition, collaboration. Technology also greatly eases the life of a transformative leader in customizing student experiences. It is through adaptive learning platforms, interactive simulations, and tailor-made feedback mechanisms that have gained the power to make instructors personalize instruction according to the interests, pace, and needs of every learner.

3.   **Strategies for Effective Transformative Leadership in the Technological Era**

Effective transformative leadership within the technological era harbours growth mindset attributes, building strong relationships and connections, inspiring creativity and experimentation, for a nurturing and inclusive work environment. Applying such strategies, therefore, will put leaders in a capacity to solve issues of complexities in their adoption of educational technology and provide support for innovation in their organizations for beneficial change to the students in this era of digital age student preparedness.

Embracing a Growth Mindset

In the modern technology era, there is no other way the building of strong relationships and networks can be considered in the transformational leadership process; it is indispensable. Good relationships have to be built in workplaces, among team members and colleagues, among students, and with the parents and the stakeholders in the community. Bringing in open communication, trust, and empathy, the leaders will have done very well in the development of a good environment where the members of a given team are motivated to work towards common goals and objectives. Educational system leaders need to be reflective in their practice which supports their professional capacity to further twenty-first-century learning environments. Interact socially with other educational leaders, experts from the industry, and technology partners by developing as many contacts with other educational leaders as experts to be updated about the latest experiences and developing practices.

Building Strong Relationships and Networks

Another essential aspect of effective transformative leadership in the technological era is building strong relationships and networks. Educational leaders must cultivate positive relationships with their team members, colleagues, students, parents, and community stakeholders to create a supportive and collaborative working environment. By fostering open communication, trust, and empathy, leaders can build strong teams that are motivated to work towards common goals and objectives. Additionally, leaders should actively seek out opportunities to network with other educational leaders, industry experts, and technology partners to stay informed about the latest trends and best practices in educational technology.

Encouraging Creativity and Experimentation

It is what drives creativity and experimentation in the professional and effective world of educational technology. It demands that educational leaders support their teams and take some minor and moderate risks in the practices of learning and teaching to venture where their minds will wander in trying new things. In this way, the leader creates a culture whereby the team gets room to tap the potential of technology to help improve learning outcomes for students through offering creativity, innovation, and experimentation. Leaders should supply their people with real resource support and the indispensability to try new technologies, new pedagogical approaches, and even new learning models to get what will truly work.

Fostering a Supportive and Inclusive Work Environment

Effective transformational leadership in the technological age should involve an empowering and all-inclusive environment concerning its workforce. Armed with this information, informed educational leaders shall always have in mind those factors in their practice so that every member of their team is valued, respected, and empowered. Really by the many adjustments in roles and inclusion that the leader creates, all of these efforts together result in a place where all team members belong, with the freedom to openly share ideas, voice concerns, and celebrate success without limits or fears. Such a leader also ensures the team members or followers receive feedback, be it positive or negative, and thus are in a position to celebrate success and make the working environment conducive.

4.   Future Trends in Technology and Leadership

The integration of technology into future educational leadership sums up great potential for transforming policy, practice, and student learning. Re-imagining critical leading trends in artificial intelligence, virtual and augmented reality, and consideration for ethics, among others, must lead educational leaders to craft a more vibrant and inclusive education to prepare students in the best ways possible and ensure success. In a digital age, overall, the general drifts against the convergence of technology and leadership in education will be. These technology-made steps have a high level of improved and motivated development of transformative leadership in the education set to facilitate their efficiency. Indeed, there is a burning need to explore the future potential trends in technology and leadership pegged into changing the landscape in which education is taking place in years to come.

Artificial Intelligence in Education

The cutting edge of educational technology is just a puddle of possible uses let in by artificial intelligence (AI) in data analysis, enhancements to organizational functions, and teacher and student learning experiences. Other than ease added to the processes of education, predictive analysis, automated grading systems, and intelligent tutoring systems are also able to step up in the process of improving teaching and thus satisfying the unique needs of a student. The promise of AI is said to allow educational leaders to creep into an even more responsive and adaptive learning environment toward their greatest potential to involve a learner. Second, the way traditional educational content was formed, shared, and estimated might change. For example, AI can make assessments of an enormous number of complex datasets to give judgment regarding patterns and critical areas that will speak volumes about the kind of curriculum, and instructional design approach, through the use of machine learning algorithms. Moreover, AI-infused chatbots or virtual assistants can provide real-time facilitation to both learners and educators with a 360-degree feedback mechanism just as per their tailor-made inputs.

Virtual and Augmented Reality Applications

With the technologies of virtual and augmented reality (AV/AR) coming up, learners are entitled to get experiences typical, highly interactive, intuitive, and above all immersive. It goes further up and above what would be done within the four walls of the classroom, hence easier engagement of students. AR/VR applications enable them to learn tough concepts, provide spaces to conduct experiments, and a place in which to collaborate in a dynamically engaging environment with peers. With these technologies, educational leaders can be assured of substantial improvement in learning experiences that are tailor-made to fit individualized styles and to raise creativity together with the ability for critical thinking. The possibility for creation is endless. Virtual and augmented reality can also totally blur the boundary of theory with practice that is at zero, offering students a chance to completely experience the application of their theoretical knowledge in practice and develop practical skills in several areas. From virtual field trips to interactive simulations, AR, and VR applications, they ushered in a new phase of experiential learning, actively involved students, while living through and learning.

Ethical Considerations in Educational Technology

With technology at the forefront, it creates the very imperative questions of educational leadership over ethical considerations and responsible use of educational technology. By and large, everything in the bracket of issues that would fall under ethical considerations within educational technology needs sensitive care and proactive measures. Such an educational leader should be at the forefront of subscribing to ethical practices in working out the best way to embed technologies, ensuring the protection of students' data and privacy rights, and use of digital literacy. This would ensure all students and educators are responsible for the use of technology. Secondly, the administration should establish clear guidelines and policies that subscribe to ethical standards and values for the learning environment as secure and safe for all. Ethically, the rise of the use of technology in education has to be carefully considered as it is integrated into the learning landscape on the rise. It will require educators to consider, very reflectively, the ethical considerations of data privacy, issues regarding digital equity, and even probable algorithmic bias in its adoption. In that way, it is upon the educators and leaders to treasure their stability and influence through such moral obstacles by aiding the learners to learn how to responsibly use technology and finally grow. This is significant since concerning educational leadership, the future can be shaped where technology will be showcasing a tool that brings about change to benefit the good of education through the promotion of digital literacy, the creation of an ethos for equitable use of technology, and placement with the best interest of the student at the centre.

Chapter 8: Community Engagement and Partnerships

Community engagement and partnerships play a crucial role in improving educational outcomes and fostering a supportive learning environment for students. When schools, families, communities, and other stakeholders work together collaboratively, they can create a more holistic and inclusive approach to education that addresses the diverse needs and aspirations of students. Here's a detailed exploration of community engagement and partnerships for education:

Importance of Community Engagement and Partnerships:

Holistic Support: Community engagement and partnerships allow schools to access a wide range of resources, expertise, and support services that can address the various academic, social, emotional, and physical needs of students.

Cultural Responsiveness: Engaging with diverse communities helps schools better understand and respond to the cultural, linguistic, and socio-economic backgrounds of their students and families, creating a more inclusive and culturally responsive learning environment.

Shared Responsibility: By involving families, community organizations, businesses, and other stakeholders in education, schools can foster a sense of shared responsibility for student success, leading to greater accountability, collaboration, and support for educational initiatives.

Enhanced Learning Opportunities: Community partnerships provide students with access to a wider range of learning opportunities, such as internships, mentorship programs, extracurricular activities, and enrichment programs, that complement and enrich their academic experiences.

Increased Engagement and Motivation: Engaging families and communities in education can increase student motivation, engagement, and academic achievement by demonstrating the importance of education and providing positive role models and support networks.

Strategies for Community Engagement and Partnerships:

Establishing Communication Channels: Schools should establish effective communication channels to keep families, community members, and stakeholders informed and engaged in the educational process. This may include newsletters, websites, social media, parent-teacher conferences, and community forums.

Building Trust and Relationships: Schools should invest time and effort in building trust and positive relationships with families, community organizations, and other stakeholders. This may involve outreach efforts, cultural competence training, and opportunities for meaningful collaboration and involvement.

Involving Families in Decision-Making: Schools should involve families in decision-making processes related to school policies, programs, and initiatives. This may include forming parent advisory councils, soliciting feedback through surveys and focus groups, and providing opportunities for parents to serve on school committees and boards.

Collaborating with Community Organizations: Schools should forge partnerships with local businesses, nonprofit organizations, government agencies, and other community stakeholders to provide students with access to resources, support services, and learning opportunities. This may include internships, job shadowing programs, tutoring services, health and wellness programs, and enrichment activities.

Promoting Family Engagement in Learning: Schools should provide families with resources, information, and strategies to support their children's learning at home. This may include workshops, seminars, and educational materials on topics such as literacy, numeracy, parenting skills, and college and career readiness.

Celebrating Diversity and Culture: Schools should celebrate and embrace the diversity of their student body and community through multicultural events, festivals, and curriculum that reflect the lived experiences, traditions, and contributions of diverse cultures and communities.

Fostering Two-Way Communication: Schools should create opportunities for two-way communication between educators and families, allowing for open dialogue, feedback, and collaboration. This may include parent-teacher conferences, home visits, and regular communication channels for sharing information and addressing concerns.

Examples of Effective Community Engagement and Partnerships:

Parent and Family Engagement Programs: Schools may offer parent education workshops, family literacy programs, and parent-teacher organizations to involve families in their children's education and create a supportive home learning environment.

Community-Based Learning Initiatives: Schools may partner with local museums, libraries, parks, and cultural organizations to provide students with hands-on learning experiences and opportunities to explore their community's history, culture, and natural resources.

Business and Industry Partnerships: Schools may collaborate with local businesses and industries to provide students with real-world learning opportunities, such as internships, apprenticeships, job shadowing programs, and guest speakers from various career fields.

Health and Wellness Partnerships: Schools may partner with healthcare providers, community health organizations, and local agencies to promote student health and wellness through initiatives such as school-based health clinics, nutrition education programs, and mental health services.

College and Career Readiness Initiatives: Schools may partner with colleges, universities, and workforce development organizations to provide students with college preparation and career exploration opportunities, such as college fairs, campus visits, scholarship programs, and career workshops.

Conclusion:

Community engagement and partnerships are essential components of a comprehensive approach to education that seeks to address the diverse needs and aspirations of students. By involving families, communities, businesses, and other stakeholders in education, schools can create a more inclusive, supportive, and enriching learning environment that prepares students for success in school and beyond. Through effective communication, collaboration, and shared responsibility, schools can harness the collective expertise, resources, and support of their communities to drive positive outcomes for all students.

- Strengthening School-Community Connections

Strengthening school-community connections is essential for creating a supportive and enriching educational environment that fosters student success and well-being. When schools actively engage with their surrounding communities, they can access a wide range of resources, expertise, and support services that complement and enhance the educational experiences of students. Here's a detailed exploration of strategies for strengthening school-community connections:

Importance of School-Community Connections:

Holistic Support: School-community connections enable schools to provide holistic support for students by tapping into the resources, expertise, and services available within the community. This can include academic support, mental health services, extracurricular activities, and enrichment programs.

Shared Responsibility: By involving families, community organizations, businesses, and other stakeholders in education, schools can foster a sense of shared responsibility for student success. This leads to greater accountability, collaboration, and support for educational initiatives.

Cultural Responsiveness: Engaging with diverse communities helps schools better understand and respond to the cultural, linguistic, and socio-economic backgrounds of their students and families. This creates a more inclusive and culturally responsive learning environment where all students feel valued and supported.

Enhanced Learning Opportunities: School-community connections provide students with access to a wider range of learning opportunities, including internships, mentorship programs, extracurricular activities, and enrichment programs. These experiences enrich students' academic experiences and help prepare them for success in school and beyond.

Strategies for Strengthening School-Community Connections:

Establishing Communication Channels: Schools should establish effective communication channels to keep families, community members, and stakeholders informed and engaged in the educational process. This may include newsletters, websites, social media, parent-teacher conferences, and community forums.

Building Trust and Relationships: Schools should invest time and effort in building trust and positive relationships with families, community organizations, and other stakeholders.

This may involve outreach efforts, cultural competence training, and opportunities for meaningful collaboration and involvement.

Involving Families in Decision-Making: Schools should involve families in decision-making processes related to school policies, programs, and initiatives. This may include forming parent advisory councils, soliciting feedback through surveys and focus groups, and providing opportunities for parents to serve on school committees and boards.

Collaborating with Community Organizations: Schools should forge partnerships with local businesses, nonprofit organizations, government agencies, and other community stakeholders to provide students with access to resources, support services, and learning opportunities. This may include internships, job shadowing programs, tutoring services, health and wellness programs, and enrichment activities.

Promoting Family Engagement in Learning: Schools should provide families with resources, information, and strategies to support their children's learning at home. This may include workshops, seminars, and educational materials on topics such as literacy, numeracy, parenting skills, and college and career readiness.

Celebrating Diversity and Culture: Schools should celebrate and embrace the diversity of their student body and community through multicultural events, festivals, and curriculum that reflect the lived experiences, traditions, and contributions of diverse cultures and communities.

Fostering Two-Way Communication: Schools should create opportunities for two-way communication between educators and families, allowing for open dialogue, feedback, and collaboration. This may include parent-teacher conferences, home visits, and regular communication channels for sharing information and addressing concerns.

Examples of Strengthening School-Community Connections:

Community Service Projects: Schools may organize community service projects that engage students, families, and community members in meaningful activities that address local needs and priorities.

Community-Based Learning Initiatives: Schools may partner with local museums, libraries, parks, and cultural organizations to provide students with hands-on learning experiences and opportunities to explore their community's history, culture, and natural resources.

Business and Industry Partnerships: Schools may collaborate with local businesses and industries to provide students with real-world learning opportunities, such as internships, apprenticeships, job shadowing programs, and guest speakers from various career fields.

Health and Wellness Partnerships: Schools may partner with healthcare providers, community health organizations, and local agencies to promote student health and wellness through initiatives such as school-based health clinics, nutrition education programs, and mental health services.

College and Career Readiness Initiatives: Schools may partner with colleges, universities, and workforce development organizations to provide students with college preparation and career exploration opportunities, such as college fairs, campus visits, scholarship programs, and career workshops.

Conclusion:

Strengthening school-community connections is essential for creating a supportive and enriching educational environment that fosters student success and well-being. By actively engaging with families, communities, businesses, and other stakeholders, schools can access a wide range of resources, expertise, and support services that complement and enhance the educational experiences of students. Through effective communication, collaboration, and shared responsibility, schools can harness the collective strengths and assets of their communities to drive positive outcomes for all students.

- Collaborative Initiatives for Transformative Change

Collaborative initiatives for transformative change in education involve partnerships between various stakeholders, including educators, policymakers, community organizations, parents, and students, to drive positive and sustainable improvements in educational outcomes. These initiatives focus on addressing systemic challenges, promoting innovation, and fostering equity and inclusion in education. Here's a detailed exploration of collaborative initiatives for transformative change in education:

Importance of Collaborative Initiatives:

Collective Impact: Collaborative initiatives bring together diverse stakeholders with different perspectives, expertise, and resources to address complex challenges in education. By pooling their resources and working together towards a common goal, stakeholders can achieve greater impact and sustainability than they could individually.

Systems Change: Collaborative initiatives aim to drive systemic change in education by addressing root causes and structural barriers to student success. By engaging with multiple levels of the education system, from classrooms to policy-making bodies, these initiatives seek to create lasting improvements that benefit all students.

Innovation and Experimentation: Collaborative initiatives provide a platform for innovation and experimentation in education, allowing stakeholders to pilot new approaches, test promising practices, and scale up successful interventions. By fostering a culture of learning and adaptation, these initiatives promote continuous improvement and innovation in education.

Equity and Inclusion: Collaborative initiatives prioritize equity and inclusion in education by addressing disparities in access, opportunity, and outcomes for marginalized and underserved students. By centering the needs and voices of historically marginalized communities, these initiatives work towards creating a more just and equitable education system.

Key Components of Collaborative Initiatives:

Shared Vision and Goals: Collaborative initiatives begin with the development of a shared vision and goals that reflect the collective aspirations of stakeholders. This shared vision provides a unifying framework for collaboration and guides the direction of the initiative.

Partnership Building: Collaborative initiatives involve building partnerships and coalitions among diverse stakeholders, including educators, policymakers, community organizations, parents, and students. These partnerships leverage the strengths, expertise, and resources of each stakeholder group to achieve common objectives.

Data and Evidence: Collaborative initiatives rely on data and evidence to inform decision-making, measure progress, and evaluate the impact of interventions. By collecting and analyzing data on student outcomes, program effectiveness, and systemic challenges, stakeholders can make informed decisions and drive continuous improvement.

Community Engagement: Collaborative initiatives prioritize community engagement and participation, ensuring that the voices and perspectives of students, families, and community members are heard and valued. By engaging with the community, stakeholders can build trust, foster ownership, and co-create solutions that address local needs and priorities.

Policy and Advocacy: Collaborative initiatives often involve policy advocacy and systems change efforts aimed at addressing structural barriers to student success. By advocating for policy reforms, funding priorities, and institutional changes, stakeholders can create a policy environment that supports transformative change in education.

Capacity Building: Collaborative initiatives invest in capacity building and professional development for educators, leaders, and other stakeholders to build the knowledge, skills, and competencies needed to drive transformative change in education. By investing in human capital, stakeholders can sustain and scale up successful interventions over time.

Examples of Collaborative Initiatives for Transformative Change:

Community Schools: Community schools are a collaborative initiative that brings together schools, families, community organizations, and other stakeholders to provide comprehensive support services for students and families. These schools offer a range of services, including healthcare, mental health counseling, academic support, and enrichment programs, to address the holistic needs of students and promote academic success.

Collective Impact Initiatives: Collective impact initiatives are collaborative efforts that bring together stakeholders from multiple sectors to address complex social challenges, including education. These initiatives use a structured approach to collaboration, including a common agenda, shared measurement systems, mutually reinforcing activities, continuous communication, and backbone support organizations, to achieve collective goals and drive systemic change.

Partnerships for College and Career Readiness: Partnerships between schools, colleges, businesses, and community organizations are collaborative initiatives aimed at preparing students for college and career success. These partnerships provide students with access to internships, job shadowing opportunities, career exploration programs, and other experiences that help them develop the knowledge, skills, and competencies needed for success in the 21st-century workforce.

Equity and Inclusion Initiatives: Equity and inclusion initiatives are collaborative efforts aimed at addressing disparities in access, opportunity, and outcomes for marginalized and underserved students. These initiatives prioritize equity in education policy, practice, and resource allocation, and work to dismantle systemic barriers to student success.

Conclusion:

Collaborative initiatives for transformative change in education bring together diverse stakeholders to address complex challenges, promote innovation, and foster equity and inclusion in education. By building partnerships, leveraging data and evidence, engaging with the community, and advocating for policy change, stakeholders can drive systemic improvements that benefit all students and create a more just and equitable education system. Through collaborative efforts, stakeholders can achieve greater impact, sustainability, and innovation than they could individually, leading to positive and lasting changes in education.

Chapter 9: Addressing Diversity and Inclusion

Chapter 9: Addressing Diversity and Inclusion

In the present globalized and close-knit world, schools and educational environments in general fit into a microcosm of society, where people from varied cultural, linguistic, and socio-economic backgrounds come together to labour and live. Such is the colossal importance of inclusion and covering diversity within the education firmament. This is the essence of the line that schools prepare students to celebrate differences, having an environment much readier for equity, and inclusive learning. In schools, learners are given equal chances to discuss diversity and inclusion in their entire educational capacity. All learners are subject to quality education according to their interests and perspectives. This brings about the embrace of diversity in schools towards a fair learning environment where students get to feel valued with their needs covered. Besides, education about diversity and inclusion is quite pivotal towards social harmony. When individuals representing any sort of cultural, ethnic, and socio-economic background come together in a respectful and inclusive setting, they get an opportunity to learn from each other and also to develop appreciation related to diversity. This is helping not only to create an empathetic and understanding atmosphere but also to create a welcoming environment, breaking the stereotypes that might have been held by the school community, and meaningfully contributing to the progressive growth of the children.

More so, academic brilliance is what drives the point home forward in terms of progression through diversity and inclusion in education. Studies show that learners in a diversified learning environment do sharpen skills like critical thinking, creativity, and problem resolution in one's mind. When students can easily access different perceptions and experiences, schools will help ignite intellectual development and creativity in overall good performance. In addition to the benefit of the academic form, a curriculum including education about diversity and inclusion will prepare the students academically for realities existing in the contemporary workplace. Academic partnership demands that people start working with colleagues, clients, and partners from diverse backgrounds in the place of today. In this regard, the school educates students about features of respect, empathy, and inclusion, amongst crucial aspects, in preparing them as regards sound interpersonal attributes to work and perform effectively in either the multicultural world or the diversified work environment. Therefore, the diversity-inclusive curriculum in education should preach the gospel of leading towards a more just society. Through inclusive practices in schools and the curriculum, schools have their prime role of leading future citizens into being responsible and caring individuals. Inclusive actions in schools, through curriculum, empower children to be the change agents of diversity and equity for the school environment, community, and at large.

Exploring the Understanding of Diversity in Education

Inclusive education means more than just identifying differences; it means appreciating and celebrating the enormous variety that the great multiplicity of individual backgrounds, cultures, abilities, and identities represent inside that learning environment. The respect for diversity within the inclusive environment sets a pace for a rich and just learning environment for the learners. It calls for leaders in the field of education to be well conversant with diversity and what it means to have an all-inclusive learning set-up. Diversity in education can be termed as the great difference that exists among learners transversely in a place of learning. The variances may comprise but are not limited to, race, ethnicity, gender, economic class, linguistic background, religion, sexual orientation, and abilities. Embracing diversity simply means taking into consideration different attributes and respect enough by making an attribute that fosters the spirit of belongingness and inclusivity to every other individual, irrespective of the conditions fastened towards him. This means the design for learning and surrounding environment in which all value, respect, and feel empowered towards their academic and personal success. The diversity in the educational environment exists in different dimensions adding value and involving complexity in the learning environment. Recognizing and valuing diversity in education means building an environment that assures equity for all people to fit into, an environment where all individuals will develop respect, support, and power to succeed. In other words, it is open hospitality toward all the experience and knowledge that can be drawn from individuals who come from different backgrounds and perspectives. Therefore, respect for and value diversity should be integrated into a school mission statement to ensure an even educational environment. Common diversities in schools and classrooms include:

Cultural Diversity: Cultural diversity implies different customs, traditions, beliefs, and practices of diversified cultural groups within the environment setting of learning, showing in them elements such as language, food, clothing, rituals, and celebrations. Embracing cultural diversity in education includes, therefore, learning from diverse perspectives, intercultural appreciation among learners, cultural events and holidays, and, of course, the learning environment with cultural inclusivity.

Linguistic Diversity: Linguistic diversity underlines the various languages that are possible in the school's program, especially by multilingual or diversely distinguished students. Linguistic diversity is the recognition of languages other than English as a symbolic factor in education that learners at schools are learning a second language, that they are also speakers of some other language, and that languages should be valued and maintained.

Neurodiversity: This means that neurodiversity seeks to include the whole variety of differences in the neuronal range and activity found not only among people but more specifically among people who are autistic, with attention deficit hyperactivity disorder and dyslexic. That, therefore, means if neurodiversity is to be included in the classroom setup, then there should be some appreciation of diversities existing in the neurodivergent classroom to enhance strategies for their merits.

Socioeconomic Diversity: Socioeconomic diversity is a difference in income, social status, and access to resources between students and their entire families. The recognition of diversity is not only concerned with the socio-economic status but also concerned with the need for educational opportunities and educational outcomes for the learners. In accommodational diversity, it is the creation of practices which befall a range of students from diverse economic backgrounds.

Gender and Sexual Orientation Diversity: Gender and sexual orientation diversity recognize a great many identities and expressions related to gender and sexuality found between students, educators, and staff. The development of an inclusive environment for gender and sexual orientation diversity will recognize these aspects of diversity towards respect, acceptance, and promotion of equality for all people, rather than just the people who conform to norms based on gender identities and sexual orientations. At the same time, it should fight against prejudices and discrimination based on any of the above as well.

Exploring the Understanding of Inclusion in Education

The process of changing the leadership picture entails the understanding of the concept of inclusion in an educational setting so that one can identify diversity and get opportunities which are equitable for all learners. In simpler terms, inclusion in education describes the idea that students from any background, ability, or other forms of difference have a right to enjoy the same opportunities for learning and being engaged in other educational activities. It means that an individual is entitled to get quality education at the level of the person and that needs to be characterized by strengths and weaknesses. For this reason, inclusion has gone above integration or placement alone. It critically emphasizes active participation, membership, and the sense of being part of the community within and around the learning institution. This kind of education is not meant only for children with disabilities or those who lack special needs in education. It goes further and includes race, ethnicity, class, language, and culture. Based on this observation, an inclusive educational setting is dominated by diversity and differences and says okay to belonging with mutual respect between the members. Most of the visions of leaders have been shaped by addressing diversity and inclusion, which focuses on seeking equitable opportunities for all learners within educational settings. Various principles guide the practice of inclusive education, and all of them contain key guiding principles known to underlie supportive and welcoming environments for learning:

Equity and Access: Equity forms an important core to inclusive education. This means having in place the required resources and support equally for all the other learners in their diversity to make it in their learning. It is about recognizing and dropping the barriers these could be physical, social, or academic from learning and involvement. Consistent support of more equitable practices on the part of educational leaders may then help to shape institutions and help broadly in the tackling of systemic unfairness for all students alike.

Diversity and Respect for Differences: Inclusive education recognizes diversity as a strength and not as a limitation and helps appreciate and respect the varied backgrounds, experiences and views of all the people in the learning community. Such appreciation and respect for differences will help generate a culture of acceptance in an environment that feels worth living for each student.

Collaboration and Partnerships: This means, amongst other things, that all stakeholders, including teachers, have to work hand in hand with the rest of society in fostering an inclusive society. Let such members pull their efforts together towards the achievement of common qualms and share responsibilities for a strong support system that shall meet all learners' needs. Collaboration leads to strong partnerships in communication, understanding, and collective problem-solving within the educational setting.

Differentiation and Personalization: Inclusive education accepts that students will have a variety of learning styles, strengths, and needs. Likewise, the use of differentiated instruction and personalized learning opens up ways in which, when put into play, educators can appreciate those individual differences and have tailor-made support put into place to reach their full potential. As a result, personalized learning plans and flexible teaching strategies enable educators to meet the diverse needs of learners.

Continuous Learning and Improvement: Successful student inclusion is a dynamic process of reflection, learning, and continuous adaptation. Leading educators stay current, seek current professionalized development, and consult in analyzing such data that may create fruitful experiences for success with support for a student. With such a culture of constant improvement, our learning environment is to be highly responsive and inclusive, thus giving room for students to enjoy learning.

Embracing Diversity and Inclusion in Education: Strategies for Promoting Equity

The embracement of diversity and integration further enriched an educational experience and bred a generation of empathic adroitly made ready to contribute to value addition in a diversified world. Transformational leadership calls for education that one must be committed to promoting diversity and inclusion. Educational leadership maintains a culture of equity and respect through appropriate learning conditions of any learning institution that include the use of inclusive policies and practices, professional development of educators, and involving learners with the family and community. For example, diverse and inclusive learning environments that nurture the learning process are sensitive and socially conscious individuals with the right perspectives to benefit from the dynamic world. Therefore, the leadership are noted for the appeal toward a boundless commitment to this cause diversity and inclusion. Such a culture would be described as centred on equality and respect for everyone. An inclusive policy with good practice collaboration with families and communities has the possibility of emerging from such a culture, which is described as centred on equality and respect toward every person. The above explanation makes it inherent that educationists as well as other education leaders must remain on the frontier of realizing this noble dream and take a proactive approach towards its realization by embracing diverse and inclusive accommodations in every level of the education ecosystem.

Creating Inclusive Policies and Practices

The major pillar of diversity and inclusion in education is the adoption of policies and practices that have an inclusive framework within an educational institution. The combination of policy and framework within an education institution has to be developed and alluded to grounds that underscore equity, respect, and fairness for every other person regardless of their origin. Educational leaders work as a team and in policy development that allays all issues ascribable to access representation and cultural responsiveness. The leadership of the institution should, therefore, represent inclusivity policies and practices to stand for the educational leaders of this institution so that all people across the learning community feel fully included and supported.

Professional Development for Educators

Professional Development is all about gaining learning on how to build knowledge, skills, and attitudes in bringing up the subject of diversity and inclusion in schools and colleges. Educators should receive detailed training on cultural proficiency, anti-bias education, and teacher practices that enable and nurture a climate of inclusive learning. Educational leadership practices are the ones which assist and appreciate educators in evolving as architects of inclusive classrooms in which every student feels accepted and valued through continued growth and learning.

Engaging Families and Communities

Collaboration among elementary schools, family, and community groups in advocating for diversity and inclusion in schools' education becomes very important. Inclusion of parents, caretakers, and community members, therefore, becomes equally vital by leaders in education and, by that extension, education leaders in involving the above in the process of education to have improved perspectives in education. Such an educational leader will work towards promoting close partnerships with the families and communities which are intrinsic to a given school, encouraging them to belong and take ownership of that school community. This inclusive approach will make education richer and expand the support network for all its beneficiaries.

Implementing Inclusive Curriculum and Instruction

Other key strategies that might be affected by leaders in promoting diversity and inclusive learning are inclusive curriculum and instruction. Ordinary leaders in education should ensure that the diversified student population and practices from the disciplines are fully represented in the curriculum. Generally, educators sensitize children to appreciate diversity through pervasive exposure to different voices, experiences, and perspectives about all kinds of people from different groups and backgrounds. In addition, the needs of divergent students challenge the need for differentiation within the frameworks of instructional practices; thus, leading to an all-inclusive learning environment in which all will be able to excel.

Collaborative Approaches to Diversity and Inclusion in Transformative Leadership in Education

Managing diversity and inclusion at learning institutions can be achieved by the people who are at the helm of the learning institutions. This essentially means that these educational leaders need to do most of the work and collaborate with other associates who are the families, communities, other colleagues, and students. This is to actualize a level of respect for individual differences within an environment where everyone has a sense of belonging and an overall sense of acceptance and support. In efforts to have education institutions set up an actual inclusive and diverse environment, collaborative approaches have a great role in getting this done.

Building Partnerships with Families and Communities

The second important pillar in promoting diversity and inclusion in schools is through the establishment of strong families and communities. In considering the broad community, educational leadership may bring the rest together and develop a strong network of a family where parents, caretakers, and members of the community are related to the process of education. It can only be done in the form of open communication and collaboration by the leaders. Only through the open communication and collaboration of the leaders, insights into diversified backgrounds and differentiated needs of the student may be recognized. The educational leaders will account for the sense of belonging and ownership accorded to the education ecosystem through participation in the families and communities in the education ecosystem. This aspect further helps in the achievement of an enriched educational experience for students and strengthens support for their overall success through the aspect of partnership. Engagement of families and communities in decision-making ensures they feel a part of having to see to it that diversity within but also around the community is taken into consideration in policies and initiatives.

Collaborating with Colleagues to Foster Inclusion

Teamwork comes in to be another huge factor key in contributing to diversity and inclusion in education. Education leaders in staffing have to work in an integrated manner in line with every stakeholder, which includes teachers, staff, and administrators, to build uniform, integral, and inclusive environments. Respect, empathy, and understanding between employees give a perfect example to students and motivate them toward collaborative work at all levels. The development of professionals and continuous training on how diversity and inclusion could be handled will be one area from where colleagues might get the right tools and resources that will aid them in taking diversity and inclusion challenges well. Strategic advisory dialogue and sharing best practices breed an extended network of support for continuous learning and development. Collaboration not only establishes a sense of unity and belonging that is stronger within institutions but also ensures that the level of education institution-wide is taken to a higher level through partnership and cooperation.

Engaging Students in the Process of Addressing Diversity and Inclusion

In this respect, a very core contribution agreement calls for the insertion of students into the process, which should address diversity and inclusion. Educational leadership can empower students to take a frontline role in creating an inclusive culture. By allowing students opportunities to air their views, share experiences, and provide vital dialogue, a sense of ownership and responsibility is inculcated. There are some initiators to these activities such as the diversity clubs in the student community. Some of these activities include dramatic functions which are usually a student initiative in process and accordance to the acknowledgement of diversity in the world, hence the creation of a culture of existence and appreciation for all cultures. This makes students academically empowered on issues of diversity and inclusion, adding value to their education and life-worthy competencies that are imperative to students in today's world.

Strategies for Assessing and Monitoring Progress in Diversity and Inclusion

Diversity and inclusion assessment and monitoring represent a complex tool, method, and strategy operating on the base of certain data available. While all diversity and inclusion initiatives are implemented, what should gain importance is ensuring the aspect of assessment and monitoring with a view of bringing about change that proves meaningful as well as sustainable. This would in every way ensure that effective means were used to keep a close eye on the outcomes from implemented initiatives and drive constant improvement in line with educational leadership approaches to making the environment all-inclusive and fair for all learners.

Tools and Methods for Assessing Diversity and Inclusion Efforts

Surveys and Questionnaires

Scaled surveys or questionnaires are some of the operation's favourite tools in measuring many educational intuitions' diversity and inclusion efforts. All this can be tailored to collect perceptions of the institution regarding the current diversity and inclusion all around from the students, faculty, and staff. In so doing, leaders will be in a position to consider where organizations are going brilliantly and from where they need improvements to be made.

Focus Groups and Interviews

On the qualitative aspect, inputs by focus groups and interviews can now be availed to further explore the effectiveness of the diversity and inclusion initiatives when screened through the eyes of the members of the school community. The latter allows the leader to fine-tune their methods according to the situation and give more of a feel of what is happening within the system.

Observations and Documentation

It will also make direct observation and assiduous documentation in attainment reference on diversity and inclusion for leaders' assessment. A leader would have a chance to see and be in touch with the happening in the environment how they are included and how this will be accomplished in the initiatives on diversity through active presence during school events, classrooms, and meetings. Documenting the progress, and more critically issues that arise, could be of use in viewing long-term trends.

Data Analysis

The use of quantitative data, demographic information, and student achievement codes in the collection of disciplinary records can help create a large and whole picture of diversity and inclusion impact. Over time, data analysis guides leaders in understanding patterns and differences and informs decisions.

Using Data to Drive Continuous Improvement

Setting Measurable Goals

Effective monitoring of the development of diversity and inclusion requires educative leadership that comes up with measurable goals. Goals should be generally specific, attainable, relevant, and timely in such a manner that the strides taken in an institution in the drive to make the environment inclusive can always be gauged.

Regular Progress Reviews

Since this is a key factor for continual improvement in diversity and inclusion, the data alongside the progress should be tracked after another given normal time. Occasionally review the KPIs for key business metrics against goals, which show which parts benchmarked well, need to be improved, and strategy adjusted.

Stakeholder Engagement

It is therefore very important that every level of management gets to factor in the stakeholders, as they will be acquired in the assessment and monitoring throughout the diversity and inclusion initiatives. When feedback is sought from students, parents, faculty, and staff, it will give leaders different views of how well current strategies work and what to change in the future.

Professional Development

Therefore, the professional development of educators on diversity and inclusion would form the basis for monitoring improvement. Through the provision of such training and available resources, a leader might ensure that the educators are aware and get the types of skills and knowledge in inclusive learning environments to help increase the diverse student populations.

Future Directions in Addressing Diversity and Inclusion in Transformative Leadership in Education

The future of transforming leadership in education lies in a place where transformation is resolutely shown to address diversification and inclusion. What this amounts to is that if educational leaders will take good care of intersectionality, develop cultural competence, remain involved in permanent equity-minded practices, and take their time on professional learning, there will finally be a clear way to make a difference in matters of a balanced and enriched school system. This trend portends the future of an education system, in the limiting sense, to learn to appreciate the richness in diversity and actively work toward the practice of inclusiveness that meets the needs of all students from different backgrounds, abilities, and identities. It so follows that the major future directions would need to ensure the full harnessing of the development potential of educational leaders where diversity and inclusivity take a central place in their leadership practices.

Embracing Intersectionality

One of the very solid directions to explore even further, the development of the problem or challenge, is that of intersectionality. Gleaning from any issue that relates to the diversity of identity, it has to be conceded: one does have more than one identity interacting. Hence, diversity in leadership education has got to go beyond asinine notions of what it may be and plumb straight to consideration of how race, gender, sexuality, disability, and socio-economic status all intersect. In furthering intersectionality, leaders should be privileged to know the unique needs facing every student, and from that, plan the individual ways that ensure value and that the student is fully supported through the process.

Cultivating Cultural Competence

One of the other critical viewpoints regarding understanding diversity and inclusion in addressing the issue is cultural competency on the side of educational leadership. Cultural competence is being aware of your culture, respecting other people's cultural backgrounds, effectively managing the interaction between people of different cultural orientations and adopting leadership inclusions. So, as in any other competencies, the development of cultural competence means that educational leadership can help to create the most inclusive and open atmosphere for students, staff, and stakeholders.

Implementing Equity-Minded Practices

Looking towards nurturing, educational leaders similarly focus on re-creations of equity-minded practices that speak toward systemic inequities currently housed in an education system. This directly works with the identification of barriers to success for the identified groups and then the knockout of the identified barriers. An equity-minded approach by definition means the equalization of resources, support, and opportunities that all students need to reach academically at levels that they desire for social and professional ranking. It means new policies, new practices, and restructured educational arrangements ensuring equity and inclusion.

Investing in Professional Development

Another all-important trend is with a future focus on diversity and inclusion: professional development investment for educational leaders. It will help to work further on the development of the cultural competence of leaders, the constant development of knowledge and other skills that would help in ensuring equity-minded leadership, and inclusive practice. Support in professional development allows school leaders to stay abreast of current research and best practices about diversity and inclusion work—in essence, how one can become a more effective leader and impact overall leadership in the effort to promote more inclusive educational environments.

Engaging with Diverse Stakeholders

Finally, what will need to happen in the future regarding ways that these diversities and inclusions in education will be managed will be that one has thought of the practice of encompassing their inclusion with various stakeholders, such as the students, parents, community members, and advocacy groups, among others. I argue that guidance through diverse voices is an illumination into how educational leaders can capture insight into deeper divergent needs of those communities and put priorities strategically. In other words, diverse data dimensions can affect more all-around, diverse, and sophisticated insights, hence contributing to decisions that are holistic in a manner that is sensitive to the different needs of the student heads.

Chapter 10: Policy Implications for Transformative Leadership

Transformative leadership in education is essential for driving positive change and achieving sustainable development goals. When examining its policy implications in cases from India and Nigeria, it's crucial to consider the unique socio-economic, cultural, and political contexts of each country.

Cases from India:

Policy Alignment with National Education Goals: India has been undergoing significant reforms in its education sector, including the National Education Policy (NEP) 2020. Transformative leadership should align with such policies, emphasizing holistic education, skill development, and inclusivity.

Infrastructure Development: Transformative leaders need to prioritize infrastructure development to bridge the urban-rural divide and ensure equitable access to quality education. This includes building schools, providing resources like libraries and laboratories, and leveraging technology for remote learning.

Teacher Training and Professional Development: Policies should focus on enhancing teacher training programs to equip educators with innovative teaching methodologies, multicultural competence, and digital literacy skills. Continuous professional development is essential for keeping pace with evolving educational needs.

In India, the National Education Policy (NEP) 2020 serves as a comprehensive framework for transforming the education sector to meet the needs of the 21st century. Transformative leadership in education should align closely with the goals and objectives outlined in the NEP to drive meaningful change and improvement in the system. Here's how transformative leadership can align with key aspects of the NEP:

Emphasizing Holistic Education: The NEP emphasizes a shift from rote learning to holistic and multidisciplinary education. Transformative leaders should promote policies that encourage critical thinking, creativity, and problem-solving skills among students. This involves revamping curriculum frameworks, integrating co-curricular activities, and fostering a conducive learning environment that nurtures the overall development of learners.

Skill Development: The NEP highlights the importance of equipping students with 21st-century skills such as critical thinking, communication, collaboration, and digital literacy. Transformative leaders should prioritize policies that integrate skill development into the education system from an early age. This includes promoting experiential learning, vocational training, and entrepreneurship education to enhance students' employability and adaptability in a rapidly changing global landscape.

Inclusivity: The NEP underscores the need for inclusive education that addresses the diverse needs of all learners, including those from marginalized communities, socio-economically disadvantaged backgrounds, and with special needs. Transformative leaders should advocate for policies that promote inclusive practices, such as providing reasonable accommodations, eliminating discrimination, and ensuring access to quality education for all children, regardless of their background or circumstances.

Infrastructure Development:

Transformative leadership recognizes that equitable access to quality education is contingent upon adequate infrastructure development, particularly in bridging the urban-rural divide. Here's how transformative leaders can prioritize infrastructure development in the education sector:

Building Schools: Transformative leaders should prioritize the construction of schools, especially in underserved rural areas and urban slums, to ensure that every child has access to education within a reasonable distance from their home. This involves identifying areas with the greatest need and allocating resources for the establishment of new educational institutions.

Providing Resources: In addition to physical infrastructure, transformative leaders must ensure that schools are equipped with essential resources such as libraries, laboratories, computer labs, and sports facilities. Adequate provision of resources enhances the quality of education and facilitates holistic development among students.

Leveraging Technology: Transformative leaders should harness the power of technology to overcome geographical barriers and expand access to education, particularly in remote areas. This includes investing in digital infrastructure, providing internet connectivity to schools, and promoting the use of educational technology tools for remote learning, teacher training, and administrative purposes.

Teacher Training and Professional Development:

Teachers play a pivotal role in shaping the quality of education and student learning outcomes. Transformative leadership recognizes the importance of investing in teacher training and professional development to enhance instructional quality and promote innovation in teaching practices. Here's how policies can focus on teacher training and professional development:

Enhancing Training Programs: Transformative leaders should prioritize the redesign and enhancement of teacher training programs to equip educators with the knowledge, skills, and competencies required to deliver high-quality instruction in diverse classroom settings. This involves incorporating modules on innovative teaching methodologies, multicultural competence, and digital literacy into pre-service and in-service teacher education programs.

Promoting Continuous Professional Development: Recognizing that education is a lifelong journey, transformative leaders should establish mechanisms for continuous professional development to support teachers throughout their careers. This includes providing opportunities for ongoing training, workshops, seminars, and mentoring programs to help teachers stay abreast of emerging trends, pedagogical approaches, and technological advancements in education.

Supporting Collaboration and Networking: Transformative leaders should foster a culture of collaboration and networking among teachers, encouraging peer learning, knowledge sharing, and best practice dissemination. Policies should promote the establishment of professional learning communities, teacher networks, and online platforms where educators can collaborate, exchange ideas, and access resources to enhance their teaching effectiveness.

By aligning policies with national education goals, prioritizing infrastructure development, and investing in teacher training and professional development, transformative leadership can catalyze positive change and drive meaningful improvement in the education sector, ultimately contributing to the holistic development of learners and the socio-economic progress of the nation.

Inclusive Education: Transformative leadership entails fostering inclusive education policies that cater to diverse learner needs, including those from marginalized communities, differently-abled individuals, and linguistic minorities. Policies should promote accessibility, accommodation, and integration in mainstream classrooms.

Inclusive education is a cornerstone of transformative leadership in the education sector, emphasizing the importance of providing equitable learning opportunities for all students, regardless of their background, abilities, or circumstances. Transformative leaders recognize that diversity is a strength and that inclusive education policies are essential for promoting social justice, fostering a sense of belonging, and maximizing the potential of every learner. Here's how transformative leadership can foster inclusive education policies that cater to diverse learner needs:

Understanding Diversity: Transformative leaders begin by acknowledging and embracing the diverse needs and backgrounds of students within the education system. This includes recognizing the diversity of learners in terms of ethnicity, socio-economic status, language, religion, gender identity, sexual orientation, and ability. By understanding the unique challenges and barriers faced by marginalized communities, differently-abled individuals, and linguistic minorities, leaders can develop targeted policies to address their needs effectively.

Promoting Accessibility: Transformative leaders prioritize policies that promote accessibility in education, ensuring that all students have equal opportunities to participate in learning activities and engage fully in the educational process. This involves removing physical, social, and psychological barriers to learning by providing accessible infrastructure, assistive technologies, and inclusive teaching practices. Schools should be designed and equipped to accommodate students with disabilities, ensuring wheelchair accessibility, ramps, elevators, and other facilities that facilitate mobility and independence.

Accommodating Diverse Learning Styles: Inclusive education policies recognize that students learn in different ways and at different paces. Transformative leaders promote pedagogical approaches that accommodate diverse learning styles, preferences, and abilities, including visual, auditory, kinesthetic, and tactile learners. This may involve differentiated instruction, personalized learning plans, and flexible assessment strategies that allow students to demonstrate their understanding and progress in ways that align with their strengths and preferences.

Ensuring Language Inclusion: In multicultural and multilingual societies like India and Nigeria, language diversity is a critical aspect of inclusive education. Transformative leaders advocate for policies that respect and celebrate linguistic diversity while ensuring that all students have access to quality education in languages they understand. This may involve providing instruction in students' mother tongues, offering bilingual or multilingual education programs, and supporting the development of language proficiency in both dominant and minority languages.

Integrating Special Needs Education: Transformative leaders prioritize the integration of special needs education into mainstream classrooms, promoting inclusive practices that support the diverse needs of students with disabilities, learning difficulties, and developmental challenges. This involves providing appropriate support services, accommodations, and assistive technologies to enable students with special needs to participate fully in the educational environment alongside their peers. Inclusive education policies also emphasize the importance of fostering a supportive and accepting school culture that values diversity and promotes positive attitudes towards inclusion.

Building Inclusive Communities: Transformative leaders recognize that inclusive education is not just about policies and practices within schools but also about fostering inclusive communities that support the holistic development of all learners. This involves collaboration with families, communities, civil society organizations, and other stakeholders to create a supportive ecosystem that promotes inclusion, celebrates diversity, and addresses systemic barriers to educational access and equity. By engaging stakeholders in dialogue, advocacy, and capacity-building initiatives, transformative leaders can mobilize collective action towards creating more inclusive and equitable education systems.

In conclusion, transformative leadership in education entails fostering inclusive education policies that cater to diverse learner needs, promote accessibility, accommodation, and integration in mainstream classrooms, and build inclusive communities that support the holistic development of all learners. By prioritizing inclusion and equity in education, transformative leaders can create learning environments that empower every student to reach their full potential and contribute positively to society.

> **Curriculum Reform**: Leaders must advocate for curriculum reforms that promote critical thinking, creativity, and problem-solving skills. Emphasis should be placed on experiential learning, interdisciplinary approaches, and real-world applications to prepare students for the challenges of the 21st century.
> Public-Private Partnerships: Transformative leaders should explore partnerships with the private sector to leverage resources, expertise, and innovative solutions. Public-private collaborations can enhance educational quality, expand access, and promote research and development in education.

Inclusive education is a cornerstone of transformative leadership in the education sector, emphasizing the importance of providing equitable learning opportunities for all students, regardless of their background, abilities, or circumstances. Transformative leaders recognize that diversity is a strength and that inclusive education policies are essential for promoting social justice, fostering a sense of belonging, and maximizing the potential of every learner. Here's how transformative leadership can foster inclusive education policies that cater to diverse learner needs:

Understanding Diversity: Transformative leaders begin by acknowledging and embracing the diverse needs and backgrounds of students within the education system. This includes recognizing the diversity of learners in terms of ethnicity, socio-economic status, language, religion, gender identity, sexual orientation, and ability. By understanding the unique challenges and barriers faced by marginalized communities, differently-abled individuals, and linguistic minorities, leaders can develop targeted policies to address their needs effectively.

Promoting Accessibility: Transformative leaders prioritize policies that promote accessibility in education, ensuring that all students have equal opportunities to participate in learning activities and engage fully in the educational process. This involves removing physical, social, and psychological barriers to learning by providing accessible infrastructure, assistive technologies, and inclusive teaching practices. Schools should be designed and equipped to accommodate students with disabilities, ensuring wheelchair accessibility, ramps, elevators, and other facilities that facilitate mobility and independence.

Accommodating Diverse Learning Styles: Inclusive education policies recognize that students learn in different ways and at different paces. Transformative leaders promote pedagogical approaches that accommodate diverse learning styles, preferences, and abilities, including visual, auditory, kinesthetic, and tactile learners. This may involve differentiated instruction, personalized learning plans, and flexible assessment strategies that allow students to demonstrate their understanding and progress in ways that align with their strengths and preferences.

Ensuring Language Inclusion: In multicultural and multilingual societies like India and Nigeria, language diversity is a critical aspect of inclusive education. Transformative leaders advocate for policies that respect and celebrate linguistic diversity while ensuring that all students have access to quality education in languages they understand. This may involve providing instruction in students' mother tongues, offering bilingual or multilingual education programs, and supporting the development of language proficiency in both dominant and minority languages.

Integrating Special Needs Education: Transformative leaders prioritize the integration of special needs education into mainstream classrooms, promoting inclusive practices that support the diverse needs of students with disabilities, learning difficulties, and developmental challenges. This involves providing appropriate support services, accommodations, and assistive technologies to enable students with special needs to participate fully in the educational environment alongside their peers. Inclusive education policies also emphasize the importance of fostering a supportive and accepting school culture that values diversity and promotes positive attitudes towards inclusion.

Building Inclusive Communities: Transformative leaders recognize that inclusive education is not just about policies and practices within schools but also about fostering inclusive communities that support the holistic development of all learners. This involves collaboration with families, communities, civil society organizations, and other stakeholders to create a supportive ecosystem that promotes inclusion, celebrates diversity, and addresses systemic barriers to educational access and equity. By engaging stakeholders in dialogue, advocacy, and capacity-building initiatives, transformative leaders can mobilize collective action towards creating more inclusive and equitable education systems.

In conclusion, transformative leadership in education entails fostering inclusive education policies that cater to diverse learner needs, promote accessibility, accommodation, and integration in mainstream classrooms, and build inclusive communities that support the holistic development of all learners. By prioritizing inclusion and equity in education, transformative leaders can create learning environments that empower every student to reach their full potential and contribute positively to society.

Cases from Nigeria:

Addressing Educational Disparities: Nigeria faces significant disparities in educational access and quality across regions. Transformative leadership should prioritize policies aimed at reducing these disparities through targeted interventions, such as infrastructure development, teacher recruitment, and community engagement.

Addressing educational disparities is a critical challenge in Nigeria, where significant gaps exist in terms of access to and quality of education across regions, urban-rural divides, and socio-economic strata. Transformative leadership recognizes the importance of prioritizing policies aimed at reducing these disparities to ensure that all children have equal opportunities to receive a quality education. Here's how transformative leadership can address educational disparities in Nigeria through targeted interventions:

Infrastructure Development:

- Equitable Distribution of Schools: Transformative leaders prioritize the equitable distribution of schools, ensuring that educational institutions are accessible to children in both urban and rural areas. This involves identifying underserved regions and communities and allocating resources for the construction and renovation of schools in these areas.

- Improving Facilities: Transformative leadership focuses on upgrading school infrastructure to provide a conducive learning environment for students. This includes building classrooms, libraries, laboratories, toilets, and other essential facilities, particularly in marginalized and remote areas where infrastructure is lacking or inadequate.

- Access to Technology: Transformative leaders recognize the importance of leveraging technology to overcome geographical barriers and enhance educational access. Policies should promote the provision of ICT infrastructure, internet connectivity, and digital learning resources to schools in underserved areas, bridging the digital divide and expanding learning opportunities for students.

Teacher Recruitment and Training:

- Equitable Distribution of Teachers: Transformative leaders prioritize policies that ensure the equitable distribution of qualified teachers across regions, particularly in underserved areas where teacher shortages are common. This may involve incentivizing teachers to work in rural and remote areas through financial incentives, professional development opportunities, and support services.

- Improving Teacher Quality: Transformative leadership focuses on enhancing the quality of teaching through targeted teacher training and professional development programs. This includes equipping teachers with the pedagogical skills, subject knowledge, and classroom management techniques necessary to deliver high-quality instruction and support student learning effectively.

- Addressing Teacher Shortages: Transformative leaders implement strategies to address teacher shortages, such as expanding teacher recruitment efforts, improving teacher retention rates, and investing in the training and deployment of community-based educators and para-teachers to supplement the existing teaching workforce.

Community Engagement and Empowerment:

- Strengthening Community Participation: Transformative leadership emphasizes the importance of engaging local communities in the education process and empowering them to take ownership of their children's education. This involves establishing school management committees, parent-teacher associations, and community education forums to facilitate dialogue, collaboration, and decision-making at the grassroots level.

- Promoting Girls' Education: Transformative leaders prioritize policies aimed at promoting girls' education and addressing gender disparities in access to schooling. This may involve implementing targeted interventions such as scholarships, girls' mentorship programs, menstrual hygiene management initiatives, and community sensitization campaigns to overcome cultural barriers and social norms that hinder girls' education.

- Addressing Socio-economic Factors: Transformative leadership recognizes the interconnectedness of education and socio-economic development and prioritizes policies that address underlying factors contributing to educational disparities, such as poverty, inequality, and social exclusion. This may involve implementing poverty alleviation programs, providing socio-economic support to vulnerable families, and creating pathways for disadvantaged children to access education, including scholarships, school feeding programs, and financial assistance.

In conclusion, transformative leadership in education in Nigeria should prioritize policies aimed at reducing educational disparities through targeted interventions such as infrastructure development, teacher recruitment and training, and community engagement. By addressing the root causes of educational inequality and ensuring that all children have equal opportunities to access a quality education, transformative leaders can contribute to the socio-economic development and prosperity of the nation.

Curbing Corruption and Mismanagement: Corruption and mismanagement are pervasive challenges in Nigeria's education sector, undermining its effectiveness and eroding public trust. Transformative leaders must implement policies to enhance transparency, accountability, and integrity in educational governance and resource allocation.

Curbing corruption and mismanagement in Nigeria's education sector is crucial for ensuring the effective delivery of quality education, promoting equitable access, and rebuilding public trust in the system. Transformative leadership recognizes that corruption undermines educational outcomes, exacerbates inequalities, and erodes public confidence in the integrity of the education system. Here's how transformative leaders can implement policies to enhance transparency, accountability, and integrity in educational governance and resource allocation:

Strengthening Institutional Oversight:
- Establishing Anti-Corruption Bodies: Transformative leaders prioritize the establishment of independent anti-corruption bodies or agencies tasked with investigating and prosecuting corruption cases in the education sector. These bodies should be empowered with the authority, resources, and mandate to investigate allegations of corruption, hold perpetrators accountable, and recover stolen assets.
- Enhancing Internal Controls: Transformative leadership focuses on strengthening internal controls within educational institutions to prevent corruption and mismanagement. This involves implementing robust financial management systems, procurement procedures, and internal auditing mechanisms to ensure transparency, accountability, and compliance with regulations.
- Promoting Whistleblower Protection: Transformative leaders enact policies to protect whistleblowers who report instances of corruption, fraud, or malpractice within the education sector. Whistleblower protection laws should safeguard individuals from retaliation, harassment, or victimization for speaking out against corruption and promoting accountability.

Promoting Transparency and Public Participation:
- Open Budgeting and Financial Reporting: Transformative leaders prioritize policies that promote transparency in budgeting and financial management processes within the education sector. This includes publishing detailed budget allocations, expenditure reports, and financial statements on government websites

or other public platforms to enable citizens to scrutinize and monitor the use of public funds.

- Stakeholder Engagement: Transformative leadership emphasizes the importance of engaging stakeholders, including civil society organizations, parent-teacher associations, students, and community members, in decision-making processes related to education governance and resource allocation. Policies should promote participatory approaches that involve stakeholders in policy formulation, implementation, and monitoring to enhance accountability and responsiveness to local needs.

Promoting Ethical Leadership and Professionalism:

- Ethics and Integrity Training: Transformative leaders prioritize ethics and integrity training for education administrators, policymakers, and other stakeholders to promote a culture of ethical leadership and professionalism within the sector. Training programs should emphasize the importance of upholding integrity, honesty, and ethical conduct in all aspects of educational governance and service delivery.

- Merit-Based Recruitment and Promotion: Transformative leadership promotes merit-based recruitment and promotion processes within the education sector to combat nepotism, favoritism, and patronage. Policies should establish clear criteria, procedures, and performance indicators for hiring, promotion, and tenure decisions to ensure that appointments are based on merit, qualifications, and competency rather than political considerations or personal connections.

Enforcing Sanctions and Accountability Measures:

- Zero Tolerance for Corruption: Transformative leaders adopt a zero-tolerance approach towards corruption and malpractice within the education sector, sending a strong message that unethical behavior will not be tolerated and perpetrators will be held accountable. Policies should establish clear sanctions, disciplinary measures, and legal consequences for individuals found guilty of corruption, including dismissal from office, forfeiture of assets, and criminal prosecution.

- Asset Recovery and Repatriation: Transformative leadership prioritizes asset recovery and repatriation efforts to reclaim stolen resources and assets diverted through corrupt practices within the education sector. Policies should facilitate collaboration with international partners, law enforcement agencies, and financial institutions to track, freeze, and repatriate illicit funds and assets acquired through corruption.

In conclusion, transformative leadership in Nigeria's education sector must prioritize policies aimed at curbing corruption and mismanagement through enhanced transparency, accountability, and integrity in educational governance and resource allocation. By promoting ethical leadership, strengthening institutional oversight, fostering transparency, and enforcing accountability measures, transformative leaders can restore public trust, enhance educational outcomes, and build a more equitable and sustainable education system for all Nigerians.

Teacher Welfare and Capacity Building: Improving teacher welfare, including salaries, working conditions, and professional development opportunities, is crucial for attracting and retaining qualified educators. Policies should prioritize teacher training, certification, and support mechanisms to enhance instructional quality and student outcomes.

Improving teacher welfare and capacity building is essential for enhancing the quality of education and ensuring positive student outcomes. Transformative leadership recognizes that teachers are the cornerstone of the education system and prioritizes policies aimed at attracting, retaining, and supporting qualified educators. Here's how transformative leaders can improve teacher welfare and capacity building through targeted policies:

Competitive Salaries and Benefits:
- Salary Reform: Transformative leaders advocate for competitive and fair salaries for teachers that reflect their qualifications, experience, and contributions to the education system. This involves conducting regular salary reviews, adjusting pay scales to keep pace with inflation and cost of living, and ensuring equitable remuneration across different regions and school types.
- Benefits Package: In addition to salary, transformative leaders prioritize the provision of comprehensive benefits packages for teachers, including health

insurance, retirement plans, housing allowances, and other incentives to improve their overall welfare and financial security.

Improving Working Conditions:

- Safe and Supportive Environment: Transformative leaders prioritize creating safe, supportive, and conducive working environments for teachers by addressing issues such as school infrastructure, classroom management, discipline policies, and student behavior. Policies should promote positive school climates, effective disciplinary practices, and mechanisms for resolving conflicts and grievances.

- Reducing Workload: Transformative leadership focuses on reducing excessive workloads and administrative burdens on teachers, allowing them to focus more on teaching and student engagement. This may involve streamlining administrative processes, providing administrative support staff, and leveraging technology to automate routine tasks.

Professional Development Opportunities:

- Teacher Training Programs: Transformative leaders prioritize policies that provide ongoing professional development opportunities for teachers to enhance their pedagogical skills, subject knowledge, and instructional effectiveness. This includes investing in pre-service and in-service teacher training programs, workshops, seminars, and conferences that address emerging trends, best practices, and innovative teaching methodologies.

- Certification and Licensing: Transformative leadership emphasizes the importance of teacher certification and licensing to ensure that educators meet rigorous standards of competence and professionalism. Policies should establish clear criteria and pathways for teacher certification, including requirements for initial licensure, renewal, and advanced certification based on demonstrated proficiency and continuous learning.

- Specialized Training: Transformative leaders recognize the diverse needs of teachers and prioritize policies that provide specialized training and support for educators working with specific student populations, such as English language learners, students with disabilities, or gifted and talented students. This may involve offering targeted workshops, courses, and resources tailored to address the unique needs and challenges of different teaching contexts.

Support Mechanisms:

- Mentorship and Coaching: Transformative leadership promotes mentorship and coaching programs to provide novice teachers with guidance, support, and professional development opportunities from experienced colleagues. Mentorship programs pair new teachers with seasoned educators who can offer advice, feedback, and encouragement to help them navigate the challenges of their profession and improve their teaching practice.
- Peer Learning Communities: Transformative leaders facilitate the formation of peer learning communities or professional learning communities (PLCs) where teachers can collaborate, share ideas, and learn from each other's experiences. PLCs provide a forum for ongoing dialogue, reflection, and collaboration among educators, fostering a culture of continuous improvement and innovation within the teaching profession.

By prioritizing teacher welfare and capacity building through competitive salaries, improved working conditions, professional development opportunities, and support mechanisms, transformative leaders can create an enabling environment that attracts, retains, and empowers qualified educators. Investing in teachers is not only essential for improving instructional quality and student outcomes but also for building a sustainable education system that nurtures the growth and development of all learners.

Promoting Multilingual Education: Nigeria is linguistically diverse, with hundreds of languages spoken across the country. Transformative leadership should advocate for policies that promote multilingual education, recognizing the importance of mother tongue instruction in fostering cognitive development, cultural preservation, and educational equity.

romoting multilingual education in Nigeria is crucial for harnessing the linguistic diversity of the country to enhance educational outcomes, preserve cultural heritage, and promote social inclusion. Transformative leadership recognizes the value of mother tongue instruction in fostering cognitive development, cultural preservation, and educational equity. Here's how transformative leaders can advocate for policies that promote multilingual education in Nigeria, along with examples of initiatives and best practices:

Recognizing Linguistic Diversity:
- Example: Nigeria is home to over 500 languages, with Hausa, Yoruba, and Igbo being the most widely spoken. However, many other languages are also spoken by smaller communities across the country. Transformative leaders recognize the richness of this linguistic diversity and acknowledge the importance of preserving and promoting indigenous languages in the education system.

Mother Tongue Instruction:
- Example: In regions where Hausa, Yoruba, Igbo, or other indigenous languages are widely spoken, transformative leaders advocate for the inclusion of mother tongue instruction in early childhood education and primary schooling. For example, the Anambra State government in Nigeria introduced the "Mother Tongue Plus" initiative, which incorporates Igbo language instruction into early childhood education to promote cultural identity and linguistic proficiency among young learners.

Bilingual Education Programs:
- Example: Transformative leaders promote bilingual education programs that provide instruction in both the mother tongue and the official language(s) of instruction, such as English. For instance, the Early Grade Reading Assessment (EGRA) program in Nigeria includes bilingual education components that aim to improve literacy outcomes by providing instruction in both English and the child's mother tongue.

Teacher Training and Capacity Building:
- Example: Transformative leaders prioritize teacher training and capacity building programs to equip educators with the pedagogical skills and resources needed to implement multilingual education effectively. For example, the Nigerian Educational Research and Development Council (NERDC) collaborates with

universities and teacher training institutions to develop curricula and training materials for bilingual and multilingual education.

Community Engagement and Support:

- Example: Transformative leaders engage with local communities, parents, and stakeholders to garner support for multilingual education initiatives and promote the use of indigenous languages in schools. Community-driven initiatives, such as language festivals, cultural events, and storytelling sessions, can also help raise awareness about the importance of preserving indigenous languages and promote pride in linguistic heritage.

Policy Formulation and Implementation:

- Example: Transformative leaders advocate for the integration of multilingual education policies into national education frameworks and development plans. For example, the Nigerian government's National Policy on Education recognizes the importance of mother tongue education and provides guidelines for the inclusion of indigenous languages in the curriculum.

Research and Evaluation:

- Example: Transformative leaders support research and evaluation efforts to assess the impact of multilingual education programs on student learning outcomes, linguistic proficiency, and cultural preservation. Research findings can inform policy decisions and programmatic interventions aimed at strengthening multilingual education initiatives.

By promoting multilingual education policies that recognize the importance of mother tongue instruction in fostering cognitive development, preserving cultural heritage, and promoting educational equity, transformative leaders can harness Nigeria's linguistic diversity to build a more inclusive and responsive education system that meets the needs of all learners.

Harnessing Technology for Learning: Technology has the potential to revolutionize education delivery in Nigeria, especially in remote and underserved areas. Policies should promote the integration of digital tools, e-learning platforms, and ICT infrastructure in schools, while also addressing digital divide issues to ensure equitable access for all students.

Harnessing technology for learning has the potential to revolutionize education delivery in Nigeria, particularly in remote and underserved areas where traditional educational resources may be limited. Transformative leadership recognizes the transformative power of technology in expanding access to quality education and promoting innovative teaching and learning practices. Here's how transformative leaders can advocate for policies that promote the integration of digital tools, e-learning platforms, and ICT infrastructure in schools, along with examples of initiatives and best practices:

ICT Infrastructure Development:
- Example: Transformative leaders prioritize policies that promote the development of ICT infrastructure in schools, including reliable internet connectivity, electricity supply, computer labs, and digital devices such as laptops or tablets. For instance, the Nigerian government's School Connectivity Project aims to provide internet connectivity to schools across the country to facilitate digital learning.

Access to Digital Devices:
- Example: Transformative leaders advocate for policies that ensure equitable access to digital devices for all students, including those from low-income and marginalized communities. Initiatives such as the One Laptop per Child (OLPC) program aim to provide laptops or tablets to students in underserved areas to support their learning and digital literacy development.

E-learning Platforms and Content Development:
- Example: Transformative leaders promote the development of e-learning platforms and digital content that align with the national curriculum and cater to the diverse learning needs of students. For example, the Universal Basic Education Commission (UBEC) in Nigeria collaborates with educational technology companies and content developers to create digital resources, interactive lessons, and multimedia materials for use in schools.

Teacher Training and Capacity Building:

- Example: Transformative leaders prioritize teacher training and capacity building programs to equip educators with the skills and knowledge needed to integrate technology effectively into their teaching practice. Initiatives such as the Teacher Development Program (TDP) provide professional development opportunities for teachers to enhance their digital literacy skills, ICT proficiency, and pedagogical techniques for technology-enhanced learning.

Remote Learning and Distance Education:

- Example: Transformative leaders promote the use of technology to facilitate remote learning and distance education, particularly in areas with limited access to traditional educational resources. For instance, the Nigerian Educational Research and Development Council (NERDC) collaborates with telecommunications companies to provide free or subsidized internet access to students and educators in rural and remote areas.

Public-Private Partnerships (PPP):

- Example: Transformative leaders leverage public-private partnerships to mobilize resources, expertise, and technology infrastructure for education. For example, the Bridge Connect initiative, a partnership between the Nigerian government and telecommunications companies, aims to provide internet connectivity to schools and communities across the country, enabling access to online learning resources and digital tools.

Monitoring and Evaluation:

- Example: Transformative leaders establish mechanisms for monitoring and evaluating the impact of technology integration initiatives on student learning outcomes, teacher effectiveness, and educational equity. Data-driven assessments help inform policy decisions, identify areas for improvement, and ensure that technology investments are delivering tangible benefits to learners.

By promoting policies that promote the integration of digital tools, e-learning platforms, and ICT infrastructure in schools, transformative leaders can harness the power of technology to expand access to quality education, enhance teaching and learning practices, and bridge the digital divide in Nigeria.

Strengthening Vocational and Technical Education: Transformative leaders should prioritize policies that strengthen vocational and technical education to address the skills gap and promote entrepreneurship and job creation. This includes revamping curriculum, upgrading facilities, and forging partnerships with industries to ensure relevance and employability.

Strengthening vocational and technical education is crucial for addressing the skills gap, promoting entrepreneurship, and facilitating job creation in Nigeria. Transformative leadership recognizes the importance of vocational and technical education in equipping students with practical skills, knowledge, and competencies needed to succeed in the workforce and contribute to economic development. Here's how transformative leaders can prioritize policies to strengthen vocational and technical education, along with examples of initiatives and best practices:

Curriculum Revamp:
- Example: Transformative leaders prioritize policies aimed at revamping the vocational and technical education curriculum to ensure its relevance, responsiveness to industry needs, and alignment with emerging trends and technologies. For instance, the Nigerian government's Technical and Vocational Education and Training (TVET) Reform Programme focuses on updating and modernizing vocational curricula to equip students with in-demand skills and competencies for the 21st-century workforce.

Upgrading Facilities:
- Example: Transformative leaders invest in upgrading vocational and technical education facilities, including workshops, laboratories, equipment, and training centers, to provide students with hands-on learning experiences and practical skills development opportunities. For example, the Skills Acquisition and Vocational Education Training (SAVET) initiative in Nigeria aims to improve the infrastructure and resources available in vocational training institutions to enhance the quality of education and training provided to students.

Industry Partnerships:
- Example: Transformative leaders forge partnerships with industries, businesses, and employers to ensure that vocational and technical education programs are

aligned with industry needs, standards, and expectations. For instance, the Industrial Training Fund (ITF) in Nigeria collaborates with private sector companies to provide students with internship opportunities, on-the-job training, and apprenticeship programs that expose them to real-world work environments and industry practices.

Promoting Entrepreneurship:

- Example: Transformative leaders integrate entrepreneurship education into vocational and technical education programs to empower students with the knowledge, skills, and mindset needed to start and run successful businesses. Initiatives such as the Youth Entrepreneurship Support (YES) Program provide aspiring entrepreneurs with training, mentorship, access to finance, and other support services to help them establish and grow their businesses.

Teacher Training and Capacity Building:

- Example: Transformative leaders prioritize teacher training and capacity building programs to enhance the pedagogical skills, subject knowledge, and industry expertise of vocational and technical education instructors. For instance, the Teachers' Continuous Professional Development (TCPD) program provides vocational teachers with opportunities for ongoing training, workshops, and certification to ensure that they are equipped to deliver high-quality instruction and support student learning effectively.

Recognition and Certification:

- Example: Transformative leaders work to enhance the recognition and certification of vocational and technical education qualifications to increase their value and relevance in the labor market. For example, the National Board for Technical Education (NBTE) in Nigeria is responsible for accrediting and certifying vocational and technical education programs, ensuring that graduates meet industry standards and are prepared for employment or further education opportunities.

Promotion of Industry-Relevant Skills:

- Example: Transformative leaders promote the development of industry-relevant skills and competencies within vocational and technical education programs to meet the evolving needs of the labor market. This may involve introducing specialized training modules, certifications, and pathways in high-demand sectors such as agriculture, manufacturing, construction, healthcare, and information technology.

By prioritizing policies that strengthen vocational and technical education, transformative leaders can empower students with the skills, knowledge, and competencies needed to succeed in the workforce, drive economic growth, and contribute to sustainable development in Nigeria.

In both India and Nigeria, transformative leadership in education requires a multi-faceted approach that addresses systemic challenges while promoting innovation, inclusivity, and sustainable development. Policymakers must collaborate with stakeholders, prioritize evidence-based practices, and demonstrate political will to effect meaningful change in the education sector.

- Aligning Leadership Practices with Educational Policies
- Advocacy for Systemic Change

Chapter 11: Challenges and Future Directions

Challenges and future directions for education are multifaceted and continually evolving in response to global trends, technological advancements, socio-economic shifts, and demographic changes. Addressing these challenges and charting future directions requires proactive leadership, innovative strategies, and collaboration among stakeholders. Here are some key challenges facing education and potential future directions:

Digital Divide and Technological Equity:

- Challenge: The digital divide persists, with disparities in access to technology, internet connectivity, and digital literacy skills exacerbating educational inequalities.
- Future Direction: Transformative leaders should prioritize closing the digital divide by investing in ICT infrastructure, providing digital devices and internet access to underserved communities, and promoting digital literacy initiatives. Additionally, integrating technology into pedagogy and curriculum can enhance learning outcomes and prepare students for the digital age.

Quality and Relevance of Education:

- Challenge: Many education systems struggle to deliver high-quality and relevant education that meets the needs of diverse learners and prepares them for the challenges of the 21st century.
- Future Direction: Transformative leaders should focus on curriculum reform, competency-based education, and experiential learning approaches that emphasize critical thinking, creativity, problem-solving, and socio-emotional skills. Additionally, promoting interdisciplinary and project-based learning can foster student engagement and relevance.

Equity and Inclusion:

- Challenge: Persistent disparities in access to education, resources, and opportunities hinder social mobility and perpetuate inequality, particularly for marginalized groups, including girls, children with disabilities, and rural communities.

- Future Direction: Transformative leaders should prioritize policies and initiatives that promote equity and inclusion, such as targeted interventions to address barriers to education, affirmative action programs, and inclusive pedagogical approaches. Additionally, fostering a culture of diversity, equity, and inclusion within schools and communities can create supportive environments for all learners.

Teacher Shortages and Quality:

- Challenge: Many countries face shortages of qualified teachers, as well as issues related to teacher training, retention, and professional development.
- Future Direction: Transformative leaders should invest in teacher recruitment, training, and support mechanisms to attract and retain high-quality educators. This includes improving teacher salaries and working conditions, providing ongoing professional development opportunities, and leveraging technology for teacher training and capacity building.

Globalization and Cultural Competence:

- Challenge: Globalization has increased cultural diversity and interconnectivity, requiring educators and students to develop cross-cultural competence and global citizenship skills.
- Future Direction: Transformative leaders should promote multicultural education, intercultural exchange programs, and global learning initiatives that foster cultural understanding, empathy, and respect for diversity. Additionally, integrating global perspectives into curriculum content and promoting languages other than English can broaden students' worldview and prepare them for global citizenship.

Environmental Sustainability:

- Challenge: Environmental degradation and climate change pose existential threats to the planet, necessitating education for sustainable development and environmental stewardship.
- Future Direction: Transformative leaders should prioritize environmental education, sustainability literacy, and eco-friendly practices within schools and communities. This includes integrating environmental concepts into curriculum subjects, promoting eco-friendly initiatives such as waste reduction and renewable

energy use, and fostering a culture of environmental responsibility among students and educators.

Lifelong Learning and Reskilling:

- Challenge: Rapid technological advancements and economic disruptions require individuals to adapt and upskill throughout their lives to remain employable and competitive in the labor market.

- Future Direction: Transformative leaders should promote lifelong learning initiatives, upskilling and reskilling programs, and flexible learning pathways that enable individuals to acquire new skills and competencies at various stages of their lives. Additionally, fostering a culture of innovation, creativity, and adaptability within education systems can empower individuals to thrive in a rapidly changing world.

Addressing these challenges and advancing future directions for education requires bold leadership, strategic planning, and collective action. By embracing innovation, promoting equity and inclusion, and fostering a culture of lifelong learning, transformative leaders can drive positive change and create a more equitable, inclusive, and sustainable future for education.

Identifying Persistent Challenges in Educational Leadership

Identifying persistent challenges in educational leadership is essential for understanding the complex dynamics within education systems and developing effective strategies to address them. Educational leaders face a range of challenges that impact their ability to lead effectively and achieve positive outcomes for students, teachers, and communities. Here are some persistent challenges in educational leadership:

Managing Change and Innovation:

- Educational systems are constantly evolving in response to changes in technology, demographics, and socio-economic factors. Educational leaders must navigate complex change processes and promote innovation while maintaining stability and continuity within their organizations.

- Challenges include resistance to change, bureaucratic inertia, and limited capacity for innovation among stakeholders. Educational leaders must build consensus, foster a culture of continuous improvement, and provide support and resources for innovative initiatives to succeed.

Promoting Equity and Inclusion:

- Achieving equity and inclusion in education requires addressing systemic barriers and disparities that perpetuate inequality based on factors such as race, ethnicity, socio-economic status, gender, and ability.
- Challenges include addressing inequitable resource allocation, reducing achievement gaps, and ensuring access to high-quality education for all students, particularly those from marginalized and underserved communities. Educational leaders must prioritize equity-focused policies, allocate resources strategically, and dismantle discriminatory practices to create inclusive learning environments.

Improving Teacher Quality and Development:

- Teachers play a central role in student learning and achievement, but recruiting, retaining, and developing high-quality educators remains a challenge in many education systems.
- Challenges include teacher shortages, inadequate professional development opportunities, and varying levels of teacher effectiveness. Educational leaders must invest in teacher recruitment and training, provide ongoing support and mentorship, and create career pathways that recognize and reward excellence in teaching.

Enhancing Parent and Community Engagement:

- Meaningful engagement with parents, families, and communities is essential for creating a supportive ecosystem that fosters student success and well-being.
- Challenges include communication barriers, lack of trust, and differing expectations among stakeholders. Educational leaders must build strong partnerships with parents and communities, involve them in decision-making processes, and leverage their expertise and resources to support student learning and development.

Navigating Policy and Political Contexts:

- Educational leaders operate within complex policy environments shaped by government regulations, funding mechanisms, and political dynamics.
- Challenges include conflicting mandates, budget constraints, and political pressures that may undermine educational goals and priorities. Educational leaders must advocate for policies that align with their vision and values, build coalitions with stakeholders, and navigate political landscapes while staying focused on student needs and outcomes.

Fostering a Positive Organizational Culture:
- Creating a positive organizational culture is essential for fostering collaboration, trust, and morale among educators and staff.
- Challenges include addressing issues such as burnout, low morale, and resistance to change within educational organizations. Educational leaders must cultivate a shared vision, promote open communication and transparency, and prioritize staff well-being and professional growth to create a culture of trust and innovation.

Managing Resource Constraints:
- Educational leaders must effectively manage limited resources, including funding, staffing, and facilities, to meet the diverse needs of students and educators.
- Challenges include budget cuts, competing priorities, and increasing demands for accountability. Educational leaders must make strategic resource allocation decisions, leverage external partnerships and grants, and advocate for adequate funding to support their educational goals and priorities.

Identifying and addressing persistent challenges in educational leadership requires a comprehensive understanding of the complexities of the education landscape and a commitment to collaborative problem-solving and continuous improvement. By addressing these challenges proactively and strategically, educational leaders can create more equitable, inclusive, and effective learning environments for all stakeholders.

Exploring Future Avenues for Transformative Leadership

Exploring future avenues for transformative leadership in education involves envisioning innovative approaches and strategies to address emerging challenges and opportunities in the evolving education landscape. Transformative leaders must anticipate future trends, harness technological advancements, and foster collaboration to drive positive change and achieve sustainable impact. Here are some future avenues for transformative leadership in education:

Embracing Technological Integration:
- Transformative leaders must embrace technology as a catalyst for innovation and improvement in education. This includes leveraging digital tools, data analytics, artificial intelligence, and virtual reality to enhance teaching and learning experiences, personalize instruction, and improve educational outcomes.
- Future avenues for transformative leadership include exploring the potential of adaptive learning platforms, gamification, and immersive learning environments to engage students, promote critical thinking skills, and address diverse learning needs.

Promoting Lifelong Learning and Continuous Professional Development:
- In a rapidly changing world, learning is a lifelong endeavor, and transformative leaders must prioritize policies and initiatives that support continuous professional development for educators and lifelong learning for students.
- Future avenues for transformative leadership include promoting micro-credentialing, competency-based education, and personalized learning pathways that enable individuals to acquire new skills and knowledge throughout their lives.

Fostering Global Citizenship and Sustainability:
- Transformative leaders must prepare students to thrive in a globally interconnected world and address pressing global challenges such as climate change, social injustice, and economic inequality.
- Future avenues for transformative leadership include integrating global perspectives, sustainability education, and civic engagement into curriculum content and promoting cross-cultural collaboration, service learning, and

international exchange programs to foster empathy, intercultural understanding, and responsible citizenship.

Empowering Student Voice and Agency:

- Transformative leaders must empower students as active participants in their own learning and decision-making processes, fostering agency, self-efficacy, and leadership skills.
- Future avenues for transformative leadership include promoting student-centered approaches such as project-based learning, inquiry-based learning, and student-led initiatives that empower students to pursue their interests, solve real-world problems, and make meaningful contributions to their communities.

Cultivating Social and Emotional Learning (SEL):

- Transformative leaders must prioritize the development of social and emotional skills such as empathy, resilience, and self-awareness alongside academic knowledge and technical skills.
- Future avenues for transformative leadership include embedding SEL into the fabric of education through explicit instruction, supportive learning environments, and restorative practices that promote positive relationships, emotional well-being, and responsible decision-making.

Strengthening Partnerships and Collaboration:

- Transformative leaders must foster collaboration and partnerships among schools, communities, businesses, and government agencies to address complex educational challenges and leverage collective expertise and resources.
- Future avenues for transformative leadership include promoting cross-sector collaborations, public-private partnerships, and community-engaged learning initiatives that bridge the gap between education and the broader society, promote social innovation, and address systemic issues such as poverty, inequality, and health disparities.

Promoting Diversity, Equity, and Inclusion:

- Transformative leaders must prioritize diversity, equity, and inclusion in education to ensure that all students have equitable access to opportunities, resources, and support.

- Future avenues for transformative leadership include implementing inclusive policies, culturally responsive pedagogies, and anti-bias practices that celebrate diversity, address systemic inequities, and create learning environments where all students feel valued, respected, and empowered to succeed.

In conclusion, exploring future avenues for transformative leadership in education requires visionary thinking, strategic planning, and a commitment to innovation and collaboration. By embracing technological integration, promoting lifelong learning, fostering global citizenship, empowering student voice, cultivating social and emotional learning, strengthening partnerships, and promoting diversity, equity, and inclusion, transformative leaders can shape a more equitable, inclusive, and sustainable future for education.

Chapter 12: Conclusion

In conclusion, educational leadership in India and Nigeria faces multifaceted challenges and opportunities that require visionary thinking, strategic planning, and collaborative action to drive positive change and achieve sustainable impact. Despite their unique contexts and circumstances, both countries share common goals of expanding access to quality education, promoting equity and inclusion, and preparing students for success in a rapidly changing world.

In India, educational leadership is characterized by ambitious reforms aimed at transforming the education system to meet the needs of a diverse and rapidly growing population. Initiatives such as the National Education Policy (NEP) 2020 seek to promote holistic development, improve learning outcomes, and foster innovation through measures such as curriculum redesign, technology integration, and teacher training. However, India faces persistent challenges such as disparities in access to education, quality of learning, and teacher shortages, which require sustained efforts and innovative solutions to address.

Similarly, in Nigeria, educational leadership is focused on addressing systemic issues such as educational disparities, low learning outcomes, and inadequate infrastructure, particularly in remote and underserved areas. Transformative leaders in Nigeria are working to strengthen vocational and technical education, promote digital literacy, and foster entrepreneurship to empower students with the skills and knowledge needed for economic empowerment and social mobility. However, challenges such as corruption, political instability, and security threats pose significant obstacles to educational development and require concerted efforts to overcome.

Despite these challenges, both India and Nigeria have demonstrated resilience, innovation, and commitment to improving education outcomes for their citizens. Transformative leadership in both countries is characterized by visionary leadership, collaboration with stakeholders, and a focus on evidence-based policies and practices. By embracing technological integration, promoting lifelong learning, fostering global citizenship, empowering student voice, strengthening partnerships, and promoting diversity, equity, and inclusion, educational leaders in India and Nigeria can shape a more equitable, inclusive, and sustainable future for education.

In conclusion, educational leadership in India and Nigeria holds the key to unlocking the full potential of their education systems and preparing future generations for success in an increasingly complex and interconnected world. By addressing persistent challenges, seizing opportunities, and working together to build a brighter future for all learners, educational leaders in India and Nigeria can impact millions' lives and contribute to their nations' social, economic, and cultural development.

Key Takeaways

Key takeaways from the exploration of educational leadership in India and Nigeria highlight the shared challenges, opportunities, and strategies for driving positive change in their respective education systems:

Common Goals, Unique Contexts: While India and Nigeria have distinct cultural, political, and socio-economic contexts, they share common goals of expanding access to quality education, promoting equity and inclusion, and preparing students for success in a rapidly changing world.

Ambitious Reforms: Both countries have embarked on ambitious education reforms aimed at transforming their education systems to meet the needs of diverse populations and address emerging challenges. Initiatives such as the National Education Policy (NEP) 2020 in India and efforts to strengthen vocational and technical education in Nigeria reflect a commitment to innovation and improvement.

Persistent Challenges: Despite progress, both India and Nigeria face persistent challenges in their education systems, including disparities in access to education, low learning outcomes, teacher shortages, inadequate infrastructure, and issues related to equity and inclusion. These challenges require sustained efforts and innovative solutions to overcome.

Technological Integration: Both countries recognize the transformative potential of technology in education and are exploring ways to integrate digital tools, e-learning platforms, and ICT infrastructure to enhance teaching and learning experiences, personalize instruction, and improve educational outcomes.

Lifelong Learning and Skills Development: There is a growing emphasis on promoting lifelong learning and skills development in both India and Nigeria to empower individuals with the knowledge, skills, and competencies needed for economic empowerment and social mobility. Initiatives such as competency-based education, entrepreneurship education, and continuous professional development for educators reflect a commitment to preparing learners for the future.

Partnerships and Collaboration: Collaboration among schools, communities, businesses, and government agencies is essential for addressing complex educational challenges and leveraging collective expertise and resources. Public-private partnerships, community engagement initiatives, and cross-sector collaborations play a crucial role in driving innovation and achieving sustainable impact.

Focus on Equity and Inclusion: Both India and Nigeria recognize the importance of promoting diversity, equity, and inclusion in education to ensure that all learners have equitable access to opportunities, resources, and support. Initiatives such as inclusive education policies, culturally responsive pedagogies, and targeted interventions for marginalized groups reflect a commitment to creating inclusive learning environments where all students can thrive.

In conclusion, the exploration of educational leadership in India and Nigeria highlights the shared aspirations, challenges, and opportunities facing their education systems. By embracing technological integration, promoting lifelong learning, fostering global citizenship, empowering student voice, strengthening partnerships, and promoting diversity, equity, and inclusion, educational leaders in both countries can shape a more equitable, inclusive, and sustainable future for education.

Call to Action for Educational Leaders

A call to action for educational leaders in India and Nigeria underscores the urgent need for proactive leadership, collaborative partnerships, and innovative solutions to address the complex challenges facing their education systems and unlock the full potential of their learners. Here's a detailed exploration of the call to action for educational leaders in both countries:

Commitment to Equity and Inclusion:

- Educational leaders must prioritize equity and inclusion in education by ensuring that all learners, regardless of their background or circumstances, have equitable access to quality education, resources, and support.
- This entails implementing inclusive policies, fostering culturally responsive pedagogies, and addressing systemic barriers and biases that perpetuate inequality within education systems.

Harnessing Technology for Innovation:

- Educational leaders should embrace technology as a catalyst for innovation and improvement in education, leveraging digital tools, e-learning platforms, and ICT infrastructure to enhance teaching and learning experiences, personalize instruction, and improve educational outcomes.
- This requires investing in ICT infrastructure, providing digital devices and internet access to underserved communities, and promoting digital literacy initiatives for students, teachers, and administrators.

Promoting Lifelong Learning and Skills Development:

- Educational leaders must prioritize policies and initiatives that support lifelong learning and continuous professional development for educators, equipping them with the skills, knowledge, and competencies needed to adapt to changing educational landscapes and meet the diverse needs of learners.
- This involves promoting micro-credentialing, competency-based education, and personalized learning pathways for students, as well as providing ongoing support and mentorship for educators.

Fostering Collaboration and Partnerships:

- Educational leaders should foster collaboration and partnerships among schools, communities, businesses, and government agencies to address complex educational challenges and leverage collective expertise and resources.
- This entails building strong relationships with stakeholders, engaging in cross-sector collaborations, and mobilizing resources to support innovative initiatives and programs that benefit students and communities.

Empowering Student Voice and Agency:

- Educational leaders must empower students as active participants in their own learning and decision-making processes, fostering agency, self-efficacy, and leadership skills.
- This involves creating opportunities for student voice and participation, promoting student-led initiatives and projects, and providing support and mentorship to help students develop their interests and talents.

Promoting Global Citizenship and Sustainability:

- Educational leaders should promote global citizenship and sustainability education to prepare students to thrive in a globally interconnected world and address pressing global challenges such as climate change, social injustice, and economic inequality.
- This requires integrating global perspectives, sustainability education, and civic engagement into curriculum content, as well as promoting cross-cultural collaboration, service learning, and international exchange programs.

Advocating for Policy Change and Investment:

- Educational leaders must advocate for policy change and investment in education at the national, state, and local levels to prioritize education as a fundamental human right and key driver of social and economic development.
- This involves advocating for increased funding, policy reforms, and evidence-based practices that support the needs of learners and educators, as well as engaging in advocacy campaigns to raise awareness about the importance of education and mobilize support for transformative change.

In conclusion, a call to action for educational leaders in India and Nigeria emphasizes the need for visionary leadership, strategic planning, and collaborative action to address the complex challenges facing their education systems and build a more equitable, inclusive, and sustainable future for all learners. By prioritizing equity and inclusion, harnessing technology for innovation, promoting lifelong learning and skills development, fostering collaboration and partnerships, empowering student voice and agency, promoting global citizenship and sustainability, and advocating for policy change and investment, educational leaders can drive positive change and unlock the potential of their education systems to transform lives and communities.

References

Aagaard, E. M., Connors, S. C., Challender, A., Gandari, J., Nathoo, K., Borok, M., Chidzonga, M., Barry, M., Campbell, T., & Hakim, J. (2018). Health education advanced leadership for Zimbabwe (Healz): Developing the infrastructure to support curriculum reform. *Annals of Global Health*, *84*(1), 176–182. Scopus. https://doi.org/10.29024/aogh.19

Aagaard, E. M., & Earnest, M. (2021). Educational leadership in the time of a pandemic: Lessons from two institutions. *FASEB BioAdvances*, *3*(3), 182–188. Scopus. https://doi.org/10.1096/fba.2020-00113

Aarons, G. A., Green, A. E., Trott, E., Willging, C. E., Torres, E. M., Ehrhart, M. G., & Roesch, S. C. (2016). The Roles of System and Organizational Leadership in System-Wide Evidence-Based Intervention Sustainment: A Mixed-Method Study. *Administration and Policy in Mental Health and Mental Health Services Research*, *43*(6), 991–1008. Scopus. https://doi.org/10.1007/s10488-016-0751-4

Abdi, Z., Lega, F., Ebeid, N., & Ravaghi, H. (2022). Role of hospital leadership in combating the COVID-19 pandemic. *Health Services Management Research*, *35*(1), 2–6. Scopus. https://doi.org/10.1177/09514848211035620

Abel, S. E., Hall, M., Swartz, M. J., & Madigan, E. A. (2020). Empowerment of front-line leaders in an online learning, certificate programme. *Journal of Nursing Management*, *28*(2), 359–367. Scopus. https://doi.org/10.1111/jonm.12933

Abraham, C., Kleinpell, R., Godwin, K. M., & Dolansky, M. A. (2021). The interprofessional Veterans Affairs Quality Scholars program pre- and postdoctoral nurse fellow outcomes. *Nursing Outlook*, *69*(2), 202–211. Scopus. https://doi.org/10.1016/j.outlook.2020.09.003

Adams, D. (Ed.). (2018). *Mastering theories of educational leadership and management*. University of Malaya Press.

Adeba, A., Dessalegn, T., & Tefera, B. (2023). Theory-based lifestyle educational intervention through intensive community leaders' affects healthy lifestyles adoption of middle-aged Nekemte populations: A quasi-experimental control study. *Medicine (Spain)*, *102*(5), E31414. Scopus. https://doi.org/10.1097/MD.0000000000031414

Aiston, S. J., Fo, C. K., & Law, W. W. (2020). Interrogating strategies and policies to advance women in academic leadership: The case of Hong Kong. *Journal of Higher Education Policy and Management*, *42*(3), 347–364. Scopus. https://doi.org/10.1080/1360080X.2020.1753393

Akin, M. A., İş, E., & Anuştekİn, M. (2023). The Investigation Of The Ethical Leadership Behavior Of School Administrators Regarding To School Psychological Counselors' Perceptions. *Milli Egitim*, *52*(238), 885–908. Scopus. https://doi.org/10.37669/milliegitim.1088110

Akmal, A., Podgorodnichenko, N., Stokes, T., Foote, J., Greatbanks, R., & Gauld, R. (2022). What makes an effective Quality Improvement Manager? A qualitative study in the New Zealand Health System. *BMC Health Services Research*, *22*(1). Scopus. https://doi.org/10.1186/s12913-021-07433-w

Al Issa, H.-E., & Abdelsalam, M. K. (2021). Antecedents to Leadership: A CB-SEM and PLS-SEM Validation. *International Journal of Sustainable Development and Planning*, *16*(8), 1403–1414. Scopus. https://doi.org/10.18280/ijsdp.160801

Ali, M. M., Haskins, L., John, V., Hatløy, A., Luthuli, S., Mapumulo, S., Engebretsen, I. M. S., Tylleskär, T., Mutombo, P., & Horwood, C. (2021). Establishing a postgraduate programme in nutritional epidemiology to strengthen resource capacity, academic leadership and research in the democratic republic of Congo. *BMC Medical Education*, *21*(1). Scopus. https://doi.org/10.1186/s12909-021-02557-3

Allen, D. D. (2019). Leading the Way in Pharmacy Education: Diversity, Equity and Inclusion, Wellness and Resilience: Address of the 2018-2019 President to the Opening General

Session at the 2019 Annual Meeting. *American Journal of Pharmaceutical Education*, *83*(6), 7781. Scopus. https://doi.org/10.5688/ajpe7781

Almalki, S. A., Almojali, A. I., Alothman, A. S., Masuadi, E. M., & Alaqeel, M. K. (2017). Burnout and its association with extracurricular activities among medical students in Saudi Arabia. *International Journal of Medical Education*, *8*, 144–150. Scopus. https://doi.org/10.5116/ijme.58e3.ca8a

Al-Mansoori, R. S., & Koç, M. (2019). Transformational leadership, systems, and intrinsic motivation impacts on innovation in higher education institutes: Faculty perspectives in engineering colleges. *Sustainability (Switzerland)*, *11*(15). Scopus. https://doi.org/10.3390/su11154072

Al-Moamary, M. S., Al-Kadri, H. M., Al-Moamary, S. M., & Tamim, H. M. (2020). The Leadership Authenticity of Women in the Academic Setting. *Health Professions Education*, *6*(1), 99–104. Scopus. https://doi.org/10.1016/j.hpe.2019.05.006

Al-Zboon, E. (2016). Special education teacher leadership in jordan: Current state and constraints. *Societies*, *6*(3). Scopus. https://doi.org/10.3390/soc6030019

Anderson, K., & Heenan, M. (2021). Rethinking health policy student practicums through the application of the multiple streams framework: A case study. *Healthcare Management Forum*, *34*(4), 211–215. Scopus. https://doi.org/10.1177/08404704211009231

Arkin, N., Lai, C., Kiwakyou, L. M., Lochbaum, G. M., Shafer, A., Howard, S. K., Mariano, E. R., & Fassiotto, M. (2019). What's in a Word? Qualitative and Quantitative Analysis of Leadership Language in Anesthesiology Resident Feedback. *Journal of Graduate Medical Education*, *11*(1), 44–52. Scopus. https://doi.org/10.4300/JGME-D-18-00377.1

Asakawa, T., Kawabata, H., Kisa, K., Terashita, T., Murakami, M., & Otaki, J. (2017). Establishing community-based integrated care for elderly patients through interprofessional teamwork: A qualitative analysis. *Journal of Multidisciplinary Healthcare*, *10*, 399–407. Scopus. https://doi.org/10.2147/JMDH.S144526

Asurakkody, T. A., & Kim, S. H. (2020). Effects of knowledge sharing behavior on innovative work

behavior among nursing Students: Mediating role of Self- leadership. *International Journal

of Africa Nursing Sciences*, *12*. Scopus. https://doi.org/10.1016/j.ijans.2020.100190

Azimirad, M., Magnusson, C., Wiseman, A., Selander, T., Parviainen, I., & Turunen, H. (2022).

Identifying teamwork-related needs of the medical emergency team: Nurses'

perspectives. *Nursing in Critical Care*, *27*(6), 804–814. Scopus.

https://doi.org/10.1111/nicc.12676

Barnes, M. L., Mbaru, E., & Muthiga, N. (2019). Information access and knowledge exchange in

co-managed coral reef fisheries. *Biological Conservation*, *238*. Scopus.

https://doi.org/10.1016/j.biocon.2019.108198

Bhatia, K., Takayesu, J. K., Arbelaez, C., Peak, D., & Nadel, E. S. (2015). An innovative

educational and mentorship program for emergency medicine women residents to

enhance academic development and retention. *Canadian Journal of Emergency

Medicine*, *17*(6), 685–688. Scopus. https://doi.org/10.1017/cem.2015.17

Boche, L. (2022). Giving a lot of ourselves: How mother leaders in higher education experienced

parenting and leading during the COVID-19 pandemic. *Frontiers in Education*, *7*. Scopus.

https://doi.org/10.3389/feduc.2022.1020976

Bonomi, A. (2019). Rethinking Campus Sexual Assault: We must Be Leaders in Anti-Bias

Practices, Civil Rights and Human Rights. *Journal of Family Violence*, *34*(3), 185–188.

Scopus. https://doi.org/10.1007/s10896-018-9994-z

Brahma, S. (2019). Influence of leadership on creativity in business academics/ higher education.

International Journal of Innovative Technology and Exploring Engineering, *8*(10), 2215–

2221. Scopus. https://doi.org/10.35940/ijitee.J9428.0881019

Brown, S. (2013). Large-scale innovation and change in UK higher education. *Research in

Learning Technology*, *21*. Scopus. https://doi.org/10.3402/rlt.v21i0.22316

Bull, E. R., Hart, J. K., Swift, J., Baxter, K., McLauchlan, N., Joseph, S., & Byrne-Davis, L. M. T. (2019). An organisational participatory research study of the feasibility of the behaviour change wheel to support clinical teams implementing new models of care. *BMC Health Services Research*, *19*(1). Scopus. https://doi.org/10.1186/s12913-019-3885-8

Burns, W. P., Hartman, N. D., Logan Weygandt, P., Jones, S. C., Caretta-Weyer, H., & Moore, K. G. (2019). Critical Electrocardiogram Curriculum: Setting the Standard for Flipped-Classroom EKG Instruction. *Western Journal of Emergency Medicine*, *21*(1), 52–57. Scopus. https://doi.org/10.5811/westjem.2019.11.44509

Caban-Martinez, A. J., Parvanta, C., Cabral, N., Ball, C. K., Eastlake, A., Levin, J. L., Moore, K., Nessim, D., Stracener, E., Thiese, M. S., & Schulte, P. A. (2022). Barriers to SARS-CoV-2 Testing among U.S. Employers in the COVID-19 Pandemic: A Qualitative Analysis Conducted January through April 2021. *International Journal of Environmental Research and Public Health*, *19*(18). Scopus. https://doi.org/10.3390/ijerph191811805

Carney, P. A., Eiff, M. P., Green, L. A., Carraccio, C., Smith, D. G., Pugno, P. A., Iobst, W., McGuinness, G., Klink, K., Jones, S. M., Tucker, L., & Holmboe, E. (2015). Transforming Primary Care Residency Training: A Collaborative Faculty Development Initiative among Family Medicine, Internal Medicine, and Pediatric Residencies. *Academic Medicine*, *90*(8), 1054–1060. Scopus. https://doi.org/10.1097/ACM.0000000000000701

Clarke, P. W., & Harvey, D. (1991). The Condition of Postmodernity: An Enquiry into the Origins of Cultural Change. *Journal of Architectural Education (1984-)*, *44*(3), 182. https://doi.org/10.2307/1425268

Cojocaru, S. (2023). Transformative Social and Emotional Learning (T-SEL): The Experiences of Teenagers Participating in Volunteer Club Activities in the Community. *International Journal of Environmental Research and Public Health*, *20*(6). Scopus. https://doi.org/10.3390/ijerph20064976

Collins, J. M. (2017). Leadership development in college newsroom labs: It is transactional. *Journalism and Mass Communication Educator*, *72*(1), 4–23. Scopus. https://doi.org/10.1177/1077695815612323

Corlett, J., & McConnachie, T. (2021). Delivering resilience training to pre-registration student nurses in partnership with a reservist military organisation: A qualitative study. *Nurse Education Today*, *97*. Scopus. https://doi.org/10.1016/j.nedt.2020.104730

Dehalwar, K., & Sharma, S. N. (2023). *Fundamentals of Research Writing and Uses of Research Methodologies*. Edupedia Publications Pvt Ltd.

Demirtas, O., & Karaca, M. (Eds.). (2020). *A handbook of leadership styles*. Cambridge Scholars Publishing.

Dowling, S. (2016). Professional development and the Teaching Schools experiment in England: Leadership challenges in an alliance's first year. *Management in Education*, *30*(1), 29–34. Scopus. https://doi.org/10.1177/0892020615619666

Fekadu, A., Oppenheim, C., Manyazewal, T., Nislow, C., Woldeamanuel, Y., Hailu, A., Belete, A., Wondimagegn, D., Hanlon, C., Gebremariam, T., Collins, A., Larson, C. J., Gebreyes, W., Aklilu, E., Muula, A. S., Mugus, S., Caffery, C., Giday, M., Yimer, G., … Makonnen, E. (2021). Understanding the key processes of excellence as a prerequisite to establishing academic centres of excellence in Africa. *BMC Medical Education*, *21*(1). Scopus. https://doi.org/10.1186/s12909-020-02471-0

Frykedal, K. F., Rosander, M., Berlin, A., & Barimani, M. (2016). With or without the group: Swedish midwives' and child healthcare nurses' experiences in leading parent education groups. *Health Promotion International*, *31*(4), 899–907. Scopus. https://doi.org/10.1093/heapro/dav082

Galli, F., Pino A, B., & Suteu, I. (2017). Adaptive Thinking for Design Leadership. Coaching adaptive capabilities to empower next visionary leaders. *Design Journal*, *20*(sup1), S4183–S4196. Scopus. https://doi.org/10.1080/14606925.2017.1352917

Gretzel, U., & Bowser, G. (2013). Real Stories About Real Women: Communicating Role Models for Female Tourism Students. *Journal of Teaching in Travel and Tourism*, *13*(2), 170–183. Scopus. https://doi.org/10.1080/15313220.2013.786466

Hansen, M., Harrod, T., Bahr, N., Schoonover, A., Adams, K., Kornegay, J., Stenson, A., Ng, V., Plitt, J., Cooper, D., Scott, N., Chinai, S., Johnson, J., Conlon, L. W., Salva, C., Caretta-Weyer, H., Huynh, T., Jones, D., Jorda, K., … Guise, J.-M. (2022). The Effects of Leadership Curricula With and Without Implicit Bias Training on Graduate Medical Education: A Multicenter Randomized Trial. *Academic Medicine*, *97*(5), 696–703. Scopus. https://doi.org/10.1097/ACM.0000000000004573

Hartati, S., & Muktar, M. (2019). Influence of leadership and academic culture on academic quality assurance in nursing vocational schools in the era of industrial revolution 4.0. *International Journal of Recent Technology and Engineering*, *8*(2 Special Issue 9), 95–98. Scopus. https://doi.org/10.35940/ijrte.B1021.0982S919

Herbst, T. H. H. (2020). Gender differences in self-perception accuracy: The confidence gap and women leaders' underrepresentation in academia. *SA Journal of Industrial Psychology*, *46*. Scopus. https://doi.org/10.4102/sajip.v46i0.1704

James, E., & Salahou, A. (2021). Medical Students and Issues of Social Change: Gender Inclusion in Student Organizations. *Medical Science Educator*, *31*(2), 315–316. Scopus. https://doi.org/10.1007/s40670-021-01261-7

Jiang, X., Jiao, R., Lu, D., Li, F., Yin, H., & Lin, X. (2023). A Challenging Transition: Factors Influencing the Effort-Reward Imbalance and Coping Strategies of Beginning Teachers in China. *Psychology Research and Behavior Management*, *16*, 2709–2719. Scopus. https://doi.org/10.2147/PRBM.S419822

Knudsen, M. (2016). Media for reflection: A comparison of renaissance mirrors for princes and contemporary management education. *Management Learning*, *47*(3), 305–323. Scopus. https://doi.org/10.1177/1350507615617634

Lebrón, M. J., & Tabak, F. (2018). Leading in the Real World: Operationalizing a Power-Based

Model of Collaboration for Leadership Experiential Learning. *Organization Management

Journal*, *15*(3), 110–129. Scopus. https://doi.org/10.1080/15416518.2018.1497471

Lu, M., Xia, L., & Xiao, J. (2019). Pro-social leadership under authoritarianism: Provincial leaders'

educational backgrounds and fiscal expenditure structure in China. *Economics of

Transition*, *27*(1), 5–30. Scopus. https://doi.org/10.1111/ecot.12193

McIntosh, J. (2008). *The ancient Indus Valley: New perspectives*. ABC-CLIO.

Mitra, N. L., & Sinha, M. K. (2023). National Education Policy 2020 and Challenges to the Bar

Council of India. *Asian Journal of Legal Education*, *10*(1), 7–22.

https://doi.org/10.1177/23220058221138121

Smith, J. G., & McPherson, M. L. (2020). A cross-campus professional development program

strengthens graduate student leadership in environmental problem-solving. *Elementa*,

8(1). Scopus. https://doi.org/10.1525/elementa.085

Stone, E. A., Reimann, J., Greenhill, L. M., & Dewey, C. E. (2018). Milestone educational planning

initiatives in veterinary medical education: Progress and pitfalls. *Journal of Veterinary

Medical Education*, *45*(3), 388–404. Scopus. https://doi.org/10.3138/jvme.1116-181r1

Appendices:

Leadership Self-Assessment Tools

Creating a leadership self-assessment tool involves several steps to ensure it effectively evaluates a person's leadership skills and qualities. Here's a simplified outline:

1. Define Leadership Dimensions: Determine the key aspects of leadership you want to assess. This could include communication, decision-making, conflict resolution, emotional intelligence, etc.

2. Develop Questions: Craft questions that relate to each dimension identified. These questions should be clear, specific, and measurable. For example:

Communication: "How effectively do you convey information and ideas to your team?"

Decision-making: "Describe your approach to making difficult decisions under pressure."

Conflict resolution: "How do you handle conflicts or disagreements within your team?"

3. Scoring System: Create a scoring system for each question, typically on a numerical scale or using descriptive categories (e.g., excellent, good, fair, poor).

4. Self-Reflection: Include sections where individuals can reflect on their strengths and areas for improvement based on their responses. This encourages self-awareness and personal development.

5. Additional Resources: Provide resources or suggestions for improvement based on the assessment results. This could include recommended readings, training programs, or coaching opportunities.

6. Pilot Test: Before finalizing the tool, pilot test it with a small group of individuals to identify any ambiguities or areas for improvement.

7. Finalize and Implement: Incorporate feedback from the pilot test to refine the tool and finalize it for use. Make it easily accessible to individuals who want to assess their leadership skills.

8. Regular Review: Periodically review and update the tool to ensure it remains relevant and aligned with current leadership practices and trends. Leadership development is an ongoing process, so the assessment tool should evolve accordingly.

Resources for Further Reading

Table 1: list of 20 books on educational leadership along with their titles, authors, publishers, and publication years:

Title	Author(s)	Publisher	Year
"The Principal: Three Keys to Maximizing Impact"	Michael Fullan	Wiley	2014
"Instructional Leadership: A Research-Based Guide to Learning in Schools"	Anita Woolfolk Hoy, Wayne K. Hoy	Pearson	2013
"Leading Change in Your School: How to Conquer Myths, Build Commitment, and Get Results"	Douglas B. Reeves	ASCD	2009
"Leadership for Differentiating Schools and Classrooms"	Carol Ann Tomlinson, Susan Demirsky Allan	ASCD	2010
"The Principal 50: Critical Leadership Questions for Inspiring Schoolwide Excellence"	Baruti K. Kafele	ASCD	2015
"The Leader's Guide to 21st Century Education: 7 Steps for Schools and Districts"	Ken Kay, Valerie Greenhill	Pearson	2012
"Leadership for Equity and Excellence: Creating High-Achievement Classrooms, Schools, and Districts"	Alan M. Blankstein, Pedro Noguera, Lorena Kelly	Corwin Press	2016
"Culturally Responsive Leadership in Higher Education: Promoting Access, Equity, and Improvement"	Lorri J. Santamaría, Dimpal Jain	Routledge	2019
"Leading for Equity: The Pursuit of Excellence in the Montgomery County Public Schools"	Stacey M. Childress, Denis P. Doyle, David A. Thomas	Harvard Education Press	2019
"Educational Leadership and Planning for Technology"	Anthony G. Picciano, Laura Czerniewicz	Springer	2018
"Leadership for Social Justice and Equity: Weaving a Transformative Framework and Pedagogy"	Linda C. Tillman, James Joseph Scheurich	Routledge	2016
"School Leadership for Authentic Family and Community Partnerships: Research Perspectives for Transforming Practice"	Mavis G. Sanders, Jameson M. Wetmore	Routledge	2018

"Cultural Proficiency: A Manual for School Leaders"	Randall B. Lindsey, Kikanza Nuri Robins, Raymond D. Terrell	Corwin Press	2009
"The New Principal's Fieldbook: Strategies for Success"	Pam Robbins, Harvey B. Alvy	Jossey-Bass	2008
"Leadership in Education: Organizational Theory for the Practitioner"	Justin W. Patchin, Bruce M. White	Pearson	2016
"Creating a Culture of Feedback: Empowering and Engaging Teachers"	William M. Ferriter, Paul J. Cancellieri	Solution Tree	2017
"Educational Leadership: Personal Growth for Professional Development"	Harry Tomlinson	Wiley	2013
"The Learning Leader: How to Focus School Improvement for Better Results"	Douglas B. Reeves	ASCD	2006
"Strategic Planning for School Leaders: A Guide to School Improvement Through Effective Visioning"	R. Eric Platt, Nelda H. Cambron-McCabe	Pearson	2012
"Leading School Teams: Building Trust to Promote Student Learning"	Donald B. Bartalo	Guilford Press	2013

These books cover a wide range of topics related to educational leadership, including instructional leadership, equity, technology integration, school improvement, and community partnerships.